MODERN CUBAN

UNIVERSITY PRESS OF FLORIDA

Florida A&M University, Tallahassee
Florida Atlantic University, Boca Raton
Florida Gulf Coast University, Ft. Myers
Florida International University, Miami
Florida State University, Tallahassee
New College of Florida, Sarasota
University of Central Florida, Orlando
University of Florida, Gainesville
University of North Florida, Jacksonville
University of South Florida, Tampa
University of West Florida, Pensacola

University Press of Florida

Gainesville · Tallahassee · Tampa · Boca Raton

Pensacola · Orlando · Miami · Jacksonville · Ft. Myers · Sarasota

MODERN
CUBAN

A Contemporary Approach to Classic Recipes

Ana Quincoces

FOREWORD BY GLORIA ESTEFAN

Published in the United States of America. Printed in Korea.

Design and typesetting by Louise OFarrell

29 28 27 26 25 24   6 5 4 3 2 1

Library of Congress Cataloguing in Publication Data

Names: Quincoces, Ana, author. | Estefan, Gloria, author of foreword.

Title: Modern Cuban : a contemporary approach to classic recipes / Ana
    Quincoces ; foreword by Gloria Estefan.

Description: 1. | Gainesville : University Press of Florida, 2024. |
    Includes index.

Identifiers: LCCN 2024011385 (print) | LCCN 2024011386 (ebook) | ISBN
    9780813079110 (hardback) | ISBN 9780813073392 (ebook)

Subjects: LCSH: Cooking, Cuban. | Food habits—Cuba. | Cuba—Social life
    and customs. | BISAC: COOKING / Regional & Ethnic / Caribbean & West
    Indian | COOKING / Regional & Ethnic / Spanish | LCGFT: Cookbooks.

Classification: LCC TX716.C8 Q458 2024 (print) | LCC TX716.C8 (ebook) |
    DDC 641.597291—dc23/eng/20240410

LC record available at https://lccn.loc.gov/2024011385

LC ebook record available at https://lccn.loc.gov/2024011386

The University Press of Florida is the scholarly publishing agency for the State University
System of Florida, comprising Florida A&M University, Florida Atlantic University, Florida
Gulf Coast University, Florida International University, Florida State University, New
College of Florida, University of Central Florida, University of Florida, University of North
Florida, University of South Florida, and University of West Florida.

University Press of Florida
2046 NE Waldo Road
Suite 2100
Gainesville, FL 32609
http://upress.ufl.edu

For Blair

CONTENTS

FOREWORD

No one would be too surprised to discover that Cuban food is my absolute favorite. Most of our family gatherings involve Cuban food, our restaurants feature Cuban cuisine, and when I get in the kitchen, you guessed it, it's definitely Cuban food I'm whipping up. But for me our food is also a way of preserving our cultural identity. It has always been important for me to showcase the richness of our Cuban traditions not just through my music but also through our flavorful cuisine.

Food is the great connector, the language we all speak and understand. Cuban food in particular is comforting and nostalgic because it not only satisfies our appetites; it also warms our hearts. I think it's because Cubans are big nurturers. We show love through food. If you're sick, you need *una sopita*. If you're tired, you need *un bistecito*. And if we're celebrating, we roast a whole pig! That's just who we are. And boy do we love sharing our culture and traditions with others. Emilio and I have friends of all nationalities and all walks of life. We've proudly made them all honorary Cubans and they love it!

I grew up helping my maternal grandmother, Consuelo, in the kitchen, and whether she was making dinner for the family or catering a party for 600 wedding guests, her recipes were in her head and hands . . . a pinch (*una pizca*) of this, a handful (*un puñado*) of that. I so wish that I had intercepted those hands on their way to the pots with a measuring cup so that I could have documented her recipes in a way that could be handed down generationally, but they live in my heart and hands as well. Whether it was her ropa vieja, arroz con pollo, or her picadillo, when my grandmother cooked something, you could taste the love in every single bite. I miss that and I still miss her every day.

I really love the concept behind *Modern Cuban*. Ana has not only created a beautiful book of traditional and delicious recipes, but she has also made it accessible to people who would perhaps never cook Cuban food at all. I love the options provided in the book for vegan, keto, and gluten-free alternatives. I love the contemporary photography. Her anecdotes about growing up first-generation Cuban American are funny and very familiar. I especially love that from her very first Cuban cookbook her motivation has been to leave a legacy for her daughters, granddaughter, and future grandchildren. It really is all about family.

Ultimately, our food is not just sustenance but a celebration of family, tradition, and the rich tapestry of our culture. The power of food to unite us is what makes it so very delicious.

Gloria Estefan

A PINCH (*UNA PIZCA*) OF THIS, A HANDFUL (*UN PUÑADO*) OF THAT

ABOUT MODERN CUBAN

I think Cuban food is among the best in the world. In fact, I'd venture to say that *everyone* loves Cuban food. I believe the reason it is universally embraced is because of its consistency. I'm not referring to its texture (although that's a plus as well), I mean that Cuban food is consistent. Consistent ingredients build the foundation for Cuban dishes. We often start with a sofrito. We use garlic, onions, peppers, oregano, cumin, bay leaves. These elements in whole or in part are found in most of our foods. This satisfying predictability is the very definition of comfort food. Our food warms your stomach and your heart.

Over the years evolving dietary restrictions and preferences have made Cuban food less accessible to some. That's one of the reasons I decided to write *Modern Cuban.*

To be quite frank I've always been against the bastardization of Cuban food, or as some like to call this trend, "fusion food." But in the seventeen years since my first cookbook was published, a lot has changed. I would be remiss if I didn't highlight all the great traditional Cuban dishes that, with some minor adjustments here and there, adhere to many of our contemporary dietary needs. Our food and culture are known for their inclusion and celebration. This book is dedicated to that delicious pursuit.

So much of what we think of as "Miami cuisine" is really our spin on traditional Cuban food. So how did Cuban cuisine come to have such a profound impact on Miami? Well, immigrants of course. My parents relocated to Miami in 1961 to escape the communist regime, and they were not alone. There was a mass exodus from Cuba after the revolution of 1959, when Fulgencio Batista's government was overthrown. Many Cubans like my parents arrived in Miami without a command of the language, leaving behind the comforts of home. What they did have in common was a hankering for their beloved

Cuban food. Soon small restaurants serving Cuban food started popping up. Grocery stores and bodeguitas followed suit by expanding their offerings to satisfy Miami's newest inhabitants.

For the most part, the traditional Cuban food in Miami doesn't stray far from its classic roots. But many chefs are starting to change what it means to eat Cuban in South Florida, and people are loving it! So why limit a more contemporary take on our Cuban classics to restaurants in South Florida? People all over the country get a hankering for really great Cuban food, so I say let's give them the tools to whip up some of this deliciousness in their own kitchens!

In this cookbook, I'll offer a more modern take on my beloved Cuban cuisine but I promise not to stray too far off course because as they say, if it ain't broke . . .

Cuba Yesterday, Today, and Always

At the peak of its elegance, before the revolution, Cuba was what the Hamptons, Saint-Tropez, or Saint Barth represent today. It was the place to be, where Hollywood celebrities would congregate to enjoy a little fun in the sun, pristine beaches, opulent nightclubs, casinos, and amazing music. Revelers would dress to the nines (back when people still said things like "dressed to the nines") just to go out to dinner. Dinner always followed cocktails, and dancing and live music always followed dinner. Cuba's nightclubs were legendary. The food was lavish and abundant. Its focus on local cultural influences coupled with the rhythm of the music was a match made in heaven. It's no coincidence that Cubans both dance salsa and add salsa (sauce) to most of our food.

From the decor to the cuisine, the scene was set to impress, and every detail was intended to be savored. Since then, Cuba has changed quite drastically, as an oppressive government tends to put a damper on things. But for Cuban Americans, that era of glamour still lives in our hearts and in the memories of our parents and grandparents whose longing for the old Cuba never seems to wane. My daughters and I will sit for hours listening to my mom's anecdotes about her life in Cuba. And even though her reminiscences are sad and nostalgic, there is no bitterness when she speaks of Cuba. She says her years in Cuba were a gift that gave her memories she will cherish forever.

Truth be told, "old Cuba" is a misnomer. In many ways Cuba was ahead of her time. The country was always cosmopolitan and drew people from all over the world. It was a destination. The place to see and be seen. And like any iconic destination, the cuisine had an enormous impact on its appeal. That is why *Modern Cuban* is a book that begged to be written. More than just a compilation of recipes, *Modern Cuban* delves into what it was like growing up as a first-generation Cuban American, how the stories of the Cuba our parents left behind had a profound influence on what we ate, how we celebrated, and how that influence inspired us to make Cuban cuisine our own—a little more modern, a little more inclusive, but always with a nod to the past and the engrained conviction of who we are and where we came from. Join me on this journey. I promise that the destination will delight all your senses!

Ana Q

BUEN PROVECHO!

WHY COOK?

Prepared meals are increasingly easy to obtain. After the Covid pandemic (ugh, I hate those two words), prepared food has been more accessible than ever. Even high-end restaurants have joined the Uber Eats and Grubhub party in record numbers. With just a couple of clicks on your smartphone, anything, and I mean anything, can be on your doorstep in thirty to forty minutes flat. Faster if you pay the $2.99 priority fee.

Its fast, it's convenient, it's usually tasty, it's always a rip-off—but, hey, at least you don't have to get your ass off your couch or pause whatever the hell you're streaming on, well, basically your choice of approximately eight hundred platforms. Remember "Netflix and chill"? Pfft, that's so pre-Covid . . .

So, I've just made a great argument for third-party apps but there's one small issue. There are two things you can't get on an app: really good Cuban food and the satisfaction of having made it yourself.

HEAR ME OUT! Ok, first of all let's acknowledge that Cuban food does not travel well. It's a fact. Try ordering a palomilla (minute steak) and you'll get "la suela de un zapato" (the sole of a shoe). A Cuban sandwich will never arrive all intact, melty pulled Swiss cheese tinged with mustard and pickle juice on buttery crispy pressed Cuban bread. Vaca frita will lose its crispy edges as the shredded fried beef steams inside the container. Camarones enchilados will become little curled up red rubber bands. And don't get me started on tostones or maduros that have cooled on the drive over. The horror.

Part two of my argument is a little more challenging if your quest in life is to avoid cooking altogether. If that is in fact your goal, then be on your way with your non-cooking self. Pero, I'm gonna try to convince you to make my recipes anyway.

I have always believed wholeheartedly that people who don't cook are missing out. There is something so immensely satisfying about creating something to nourish yourself or, even better, someone else.

Cooking is an act of love. You go out and forage for the right ingredients, be it at a local farmers market, a local grocery store, or Costco. It really doesn't matter where you acquire the ingredients, just that you made the effort to decide on a recipe based on what you know the people you are cooking for would enjoy. Then armed with those ingredients, you carefully chop, dice, mince, sauté, and season until it's just right. Then you plate your creation and place it all hot and aromatic in front of the people you love and they just know. They know that it's basically you on a plate. That you put forth an effort for them and that you made it with love. And love always tastes good.

One of my favorite things about Cuban food is that it's actually quite simple to make. One would have to make a concerted effort to mess up a Cuban recipe. When I competed on *Food Network Star*, I described Cuban flavors as a "pushup bra for food." While the phrase elicited more than a few laughs, I stand by that today. Any recipe can be made just a little better by adding Latin flavors. Add a little chorizo to a traditional fresh bouillabaisse? Why not?! Stuff brioche bread with guava and cream cheese for a delectable French toast? Yes, please!

Another thing I love is that we tend to use the same ingredients, herbs, spices, cooking wines, et cetera over and over again. I can't count the time I've made some new recipe and ended up with ten expensive spices taking up space in my cupboard, caking and getting stale. Cuban food utilizes everyday ingredients that are not only easy to source but are oftentimes already in your kitchen. It tends to be reasonably inexpensive to make, feeds a crowd, and is the ultimate comfort food. So, before we get into the mouthwatering recipes in the pages that follow, let me introduce you to two recipes you will reach for again and again.

SOFRITO
& MOJO CRIOLLO

Sofrito

Sofrito is the heart and soul of most Cuban dishes. It is also a wonderful condiment for dressing up a store-bought roast chicken or added to vegetarian sides such as sautéed mushrooms. This is perhaps the first thing anyone who would like to really immerse themselves in Cuban cuisine should learn how to make. This is our mother sauce, and along with Mojo Criollo (recipe follows), you will need this in your arsenal.

What you'll need

¼ cup olive oil

1 large onion, chopped

4 garlic cloves, minced

1 medium green bell pepper, chopped

1 cup canned tomato sauce

1 bay leaf

¼ cup *vino seco* (dry white cooking wine)

1 teaspoon salt

½ teaspoon black pepper

½ teaspoon dried oregano leaves

½ teaspoon ground cumin

What you'll do

Heat the olive oil in a large frying pan over medium heat. Add the onion, garlic, and bell pepper and sauté until the onion is translucent, 5 to 7 minutes. Add the tomato sauce, bay leaf, and *vino seco*, and cook 5 minutes more. Reduce the heat to low, add the salt, black pepper, oregano, and cumin and stir. Cover the pan and let the vegetables simmer for 10 to 15 minutes, until tender. Remove and discard the bay leaf.

Mojo Criollo

Mojo Criollo (or just "mojo") is essentially Cuban ketchup. We use this stuff on everything. Traditionally we serve it over hot yuca, but it is awesome with Mariquitas (page 16) and a must with Pierna Asada (Roast Pork Leg; page 86). Even store-bought rotisserie chicken is extra special when you add a little (or a lot) of this tangy garlicky mojo. Needless to say, it is a must when making sandwiches like Pan Con Lechón (page 62). But I suspect you will find lots and lots of uses for it.

gluten free

keto friendly

vegan

What you'll need

½ cup olive oil

10 to 12 garlic cloves, minced

1 medium yellow onion, grated

2 teaspoons salt

½ teaspoon white pepper

¾ cup sour orange juice or a mixture of equal parts lime juice and orange juice

What you'll do

Heat the oil in a medium saucepan over medium-low heat. Add the garlic, onion, salt, and pepper and sauté for 10 to 15 minutes. Remove from the heat and stir in the orange juice. Set aside to cool to room temperature.

Will keep refrigerated in an airtight container for 3–5 days.

UNO

CUBAN FOR ALL

Substitutions and Alternatives

Many Cuban recipes are already vegetarian or vegan, and many are keto friendly and gluten free. I will call out any recipes that conform to these dietary restrictions; and when possible, I will make suggestions for ingredients substitutions to make other recipes more accessible to these specific diets or lifestyle choices.

By no means is this a diet book. Make no mistake these are hard-core Cuban recipes, but simple changes will make some of these recipes more friendly to vegan, vegetarian, gluten-free, low-carb, or keto cooks and diners. I will do my best to provide options and substitutions so that everyone can enjoy what I consider the best food in the world.

DOS

APPETIZERS TO SHARE
AND STARTERS TO HOARD

Over the last decade, many of us have changed the ways we eat and socialize. Used to be that we would go to a restaurant and order an appetizer followed by a main course, and on occasion, a dessert. With the exception of dessert, most of us didn't really share our meals. We decided on one thing and ate that thing.

Today, restaurants encourage sharing. Many serve food family- or tapas-style. They also divide their menus into small, medium, and large plates, which encourage people to share and enjoy lots of different flavors and textures. Food is often served as soon as its ready, rather than adhering to a particular protocol such as salad first followed by a traditional main course. The result is a fun albeit a little chaotic experience of reaching across the table, forks in hand, and passing small plates around for everyone to take a bite. Some people prefer more formality, but I think it is a great way to eat and socialize.

This chapter was created with that idea in mind. Make a bunch of these appetizers with some rum mojitos and go to town!

Fried Plantain Chips

Serves 4 to 6

gluten free

vegan

If you have only had plantain chips from a bag, be prepared for flavor and texture magic. The trick to this delicious snack is to fry them in hot oil immediately after slicing them. Exposing the plantains to air for too long will turn them brown. So, you'll need to time the cutting and frying of the plantains well. Since you'll be frying them immediately after cutting them, and you'll be frying them in batches, you'll have to cut a few slices, fry them, and then cut more and so on. Serve these with the aforementioned garlicky mojo sauce (page 11) and get ready to fall in love with our famous plantain chips.

What you'll need

2 or 3 green plantains

3 cups corn or vegetable oil

Sea salt

What you'll do

Heat the oil to 375°F in a large, heavy pot over medium-high heat.

Once the oil is hot, peel a plantain and cut crosswise into paper-thin slices, no thicker than $\frac{1}{16}$ inch thick. Immediately place the slices into the hot oil and fry the plantains for 3 to 4 minutes, turning them occasionally, until they are crisp but not brown. Transfer the fried plantains to drain on a paper towel–lined plate and sprinkle them generously with salt.

Let the oil return to 375°F before cutting more slices and frying each consecutive batch.

Keep room temperature plantain chips in a resealable plastic bag for up to 5 days.

Chorizo Turnovers

Makes 20 medium or 40 appetizer-sized empanadas

Many Cuban bakeries in Miami bake empanadas, which if you're not familiar with them, are small pastries that enclose sweet or savory fillings. While commercially made empanadas are delicious, they don't compare to homemade ones. The filling in this first recipe is a combination of chorizo *and* sweet ham that provides a delicate flavor balance. I've also given you two more options: making them with ground beef, or with guava and cream cheese for a sweet version of these little pockets of heaven.

I serve the chorizo and beef empanadas with a creamy picante dipping sauce that complements them perfectly.

You can prepare these empanadas well in advance and freeze or refrigerate them until you're ready to proceed with the recipe. This recipe calls for frozen turnover pastry disks (*discos para empanadas*), which are available at most major grocery stores in the Hispanic frozen food section (Goya makes some). There are also empanada disks specifically made for baking. These are great too. Be sure to follow packaging directions. To make the pastry especially pretty and shiny, beat brush over the tops with an egg wash before baking. It will make you look like a pro.

What you'll need

2 tablespoons olive oil

1 garlic clove, minced

¼ cup diced onion

¼ cup diced green bell pepper

½ cup canned tomato sauce

¼ cup *vino seco* (dry white cooking wine)

¼ teaspoon black pepper

½ pound ground Spanish chorizo sausage

½ pound sweet ground ham

Salt

20 *discos para empanadas* (frozen turnover pastry disks), thawed and kept in the refrigerator

Canola oil, for shallow frying

For the Sauce

1 cup thick, refrigerated ranch dressing
(I like Marie's)

1 to 2 tablespoons hot sauce

1 to 2 teaspoons chopped fresh cilantro

What you'll do

To make the empanadas, heat the olive oil in a shallow pot over medium-high heat. Add the garlic, onion, and bell pepper and sauté for 5 to 7 minutes, until soft. Add the tomato sauce, *vino seco,* and pepper and cook for 5 to 7 minutes, stirring frequently. Add the chorizo and ham and continue cooking for an additional 5 minutes, stirring frequently. Turn the heat off and allow the mixture to cool to room temperature. Taste and add salt, if necessary.

Remove one package of the pastry disks from the refrigerator. (Always leave the ones you aren't working with in the refrigerator to chill. They are easier to work with if they are firm.) Working on a lightly floured surface, separate the disks. If you are making appetizer-sized empanadas, cut each disk in half to create two semicircles. If you are making the larger empanadas, leave the disks whole.

Place 1 to 1½ teaspoons of filling in the center of each half disk or 1 to 1½ tablespoons in the center of each whole disk. Fold each half disk to make a small triangle or each whole disk to make a semicircle. Using the tines of a fork, press around the edges to seal.

If you do not plan to fry the empanadas immediately, cover them with a damp towel or place them in an airtight container and refrigerate them for up to 3 days.

In a deep pan, heat the oil to 350°F over medium heat. If you do not own a deep-fry thermometer, carefully dip the corner of one of the empanadas in the oil to check if the oil is hot enough. The oil should bubble around the dough.

Add the empanadas, about four or five at a time, to the oil and fry them for 3 to 4 minutes, turning them once, until they are golden brown. Transfer to a paper towel–lined plate and continue frying the rest of the empanadas.

To make the dipping sauce, combine the ranch dressing and hot sauce in a bowl and garnish with the cilantro. Serve in a small bowl alongside the hot empanadas.

> Lower-fat alternative: Bake the empanadas in a preheated 375°F oven for 12 to 15 minutes, or until light golden brown. An egg wash will give the baked version a nice sheen and golden color. Beat one egg with 1 tablespoon of water and brush over the top of the empanadas before baking.

Baked empanadas can be stored in the refrigerator once cooked for up to 3 days. Uncooked empanadas may be frozen for 2 months.

Variations

Empanadas de Carne (Ground Beef Empanadas): Fill your empanadas with *picadillo* (page 84), omitting the potatoes. You can also use leftover *picadillo* for this.

Empanadas de Guayaba y Queso (Guava and Cream Cheese Empanadas): Fill the empanadas with 1-inch cubes of both guava paste and cream cheese. Make sure you use the full-fat cream cheese that comes in a bar.

Croquetas de Jamón, Pollo, Carne o Queso

Ham, Chicken, Beef, or Cheese Croquettes

I adore *croquetas!* I mean, what's not to love? These little fried bundles of creamy, meat-filled goodness are a favorite of young and old alike, and a quintessential part of any Cuban celebration. They are good in sandwiches, on crackers, or on their own; perfect for breakfast, lunch, or dinner. And they can be made with most any kind of meat, fish, or poultry—I've given you directions for making them with ham, chicken, or cheese (for my vegetarian friends who love croquetas too).

   Although *croquetas* are perfectly acceptable at room temperature, they are best right out of the fryer—crispy on the outside, creamy and divine on the inside. These are a little labor intensive, but they can and should be made in large quantities and frozen until ready to fry.

What you'll need

1½ to 2 pounds sweet ham, cooked chicken, or flank steak

2 cups whole milk

¼ pound (1 stick) salted butter

¾ cup all-purpose flour

½ teaspoon salt, plus more as needed

½ teaspoon ground nutmeg

½ teaspoon white pepper, plus more as needed

2 tablespoons chopped fresh parsley

2 cups ground cracker meal or bread crumbs

3 large eggs

2 to 3 cups corn oil

What you'll do

To make ham or chicken croquettes: Chop the ham or chicken in a food processor until it is finely ground. Scrape the ground meat—you should have about 3 cups—into a large mixing bowl and set aside.

To make beef croquettes: Place the steak in a large pot and add water to cover. Boil the steak for 2 hours, until it is tender. Drain the steak and let it cool. Grind the beef in a food

processor until it is finely ground. Scrape the ground meat—you should have about 3 cups—into a large mixing bowl and set aside.

Bring the milk to a boil in a heavy saucepan.

Meanwhile, melt the butter over medium heat in a large saucepan, until it begins to bubble. Whisk in the flour, salt, nutmeg, and pepper. Reduce the heat to low and continue stirring until the flour mixture attains a light golden color. While whisking, add the hot milk ½ cup at a time, completely incorporating each addition before adding the next. Raise the heat to medium and bring the mixture to a boil. Continue stirring to avoid lumps.

Once the béchamel has thickened, add it, little by little, to the ham, chicken, or beef and mix until the croquette mixture has the consistency of soft Play-Doh. Add the parsley and combine well. Taste the mixture at this point and adjust the seasoning by adding additional and pepper if necessary. This is particularly important with the beef and chicken croquettes. Set aside and allow the mixture to cool to room temperature, then refrigerate for at least 4 hours. This can be done a day or two ahead. Just be certain to keep the mixture

in a tightly sealed container in the refrigerator so it doesn't dry up.

Place the cracker meal and the eggs in two separate bowls. Shape a heaping tablespoon of the meat mixture into a cylinder about 1 inch in diameter and 2½ inches long. Dip the cylinder in the egg, then in the cracker meal, then again in the egg, and again in the cracker meal. Place the croquetas on a baking sheet and repeat with the remaining meat mixture. Refrigerate for at least 6 hours or overnight. (This can be done a day or days in advance.) The longer you refrigerate them, the better

the end result. I always refrigerate mine overnight.

Heat about 3 inches of oil in a large frying pan to 375°F over medium-high heat. Add five or six *croquetas* to the hot oil and fry them for 2 to 3 minutes, until golden brown on all sides. Do not fry too many of the *croquetas* at once and be sure to let the oil come back to 375°F before adding the next batch. Drain the fried *croquetas* on paper towels.

These will keep uncooked in the freezer for up to 3 months. Cooked *croquetas* can be refrigerated for up to 3 days.

Manchego Croquettes   Serves 6 to 8

vegetarian

While not traditional, I had to include these cheese croquetas. They are so good. The nuttiness of the manchego and the creaminess of the béchamel surrounded by the crispy coating is heavenly. These are also a great option for vegetarians. I love to serve them with some fig jam or add them to a charcuterie board.

What you'll need

4 tablespoons ½ stick salted butter

1 cup all-purpose flour

1¼ cup whole milk

Pinch of nutmeg

¼ teaspoon white pepper

3½ ounces Manchego cheese, shredded (about 1 heaping cup)

1 large egg, beaten

1 cup panko breadcrumbs

Vegetable oil, for frying

Optional: quince paste, for serving

What you'll do

In a medium saucepan over medium heat, melt the butter. Add ½ cup of the flour and stir until the flour is totally incorporated into the butter.

In a separate saucepan, heat the milk until hot but not boiling. Add the milk, ¼ cup at a time, stirring after each addition, until all the milk is incorporated and a creamy consistency is achieved. Remove from heat and stir in the nutmeg, pepper, and cheese. Place in a bowl cover with plastic wrap and place in the refrigerator for an hour, or until completely chilled.

Into 3 separate bowls, place the remaining ½ cup flour, the beaten eggs, and the breadcrumbs in that order.

Take about 2 teaspoons of the chilled Manchego mixture in your hands, and shape into a small sausage. Roll it first in the flour, then the egg, then the breadcrumbs, making sure it is well coated. Repeat until all of the Manchego mixture is used. Chill the shaped croquetas in the refrigerator to set for at least an hour.

Place about 2 inches of oil in a skillet over medium heat (about 350° if you have an oil thermometer). Test the oil by dropping a few crumbs of panko. If they sizzle, the oil is ready to go. Cook the croquetas 3 or 4 at a time, turning once, until they are crispy and golden brown, about 2–3 minutes. Take care not to crowd the pan. Place them on a paper towel–lined platter to drain well. Enjoy these while piping hot and crispy.

Fried Cuban Bread

I know what you're thinking, these people fry their bread too?! And the answer is . . . why yes, yes, we do. Although it's not fried in the traditional deep-fried kind of way. It's more like a crouton or crostini made with Cuban bread. Some of our recipes call for it as an optional ingredient, but I am certain you will find many uses for it. Like, say, eating it straight out of the pan.

vegetarian

What you'll need

½ cup olive oil

6 garlic cloves, minced

½ teaspoon salt, plus more as needed

10 to 12 slices day-old Cuban bread

What you'll do

Combine the oil, garlic, and salt in a frying pan that is large enough to accommodate all the bread (if you don't have one, you can fry the bread in batches). Cook over medium-low heat for 7 to 10 minutes, stirring frequently so the garlic cooks but does not brown. Pour half of the oil and garlic into a small bowl and set aside.

Raise the heat to medium. Once the oil begins to bubble, place the bread in the pan and cook for about 3 minutes, shaking the pan lightly to brown the bread but prevent it from burning. Using a spatula, remove the bread from the pan to a plate (do not turn it over).

Add the rest of the olive oil–garlic mixture to the pan. When the oil starts to bubble, add the bread, white side down, to the pan and cook for 3 to 4 minutes, shaking the pan lightly to brown the bread but prevent it from burning.

Taste the fried bread and sprinkle with additional salt, if necessary.

Fritters Three Ways

Cubans are big on fritters, basically because, let's be honest, we're big on frying. Here, I've given you three variations on the fritter theme—cod, corn, and *malanga.* They are all super easy to make and undeniably delicious. Give me a cold beer and these delicious fritters, and I am one happy Cuban!

Frituras de Bacalao

Cod Fritters
Serves 6 to 8

What you'll need

1 pound salt cod

4 large eggs, beaten

6 tablespoons all-purpose flour

1 teaspoon baking powder

3 tablespoons grated white onion

2 tablespoons minced fresh parsley

¼ teaspoon white pepper

½ teaspoon sweet or smoked paprika

2 to 3 cups corn oil

Hot sauce, for serving

Lime wedges, for serving

What you'll do

Place the cod in a large bowl and add enough water to cover. Soak the cod at room temperature for 10 to 12 hours, changing the water frequently.

Place the cod in a large pot and add enough water to cover. Bring to a boil and boil for 1 hour over medium-high heat, adding more water as necessary to cover the fish. Transfer the cod to a plate and set aside to cool.

Pick out any bones from the cod, then chop the fish finely. Set aside.

Combine the eggs, flour, baking powder, onion, parsley, white pepper, and paprika in a large bowl and mix well. Add the cod and mix until it is fully incorporated into the batter.

In a large heavy pot, heat 2 to 3 inches of oil to about 375°F over medium-high heat.

Drop the batter by heaping tablespoons into the hot oil; the fritters should puff up a little. Fry for about 4 minutes, turning the fritters when the edges look golden, after about 2 minutes. Transfer the fritters to a paper towel–lined plate and serve immediately with hot sauce and lime wedges.

Cooked fritters can be stored in the refrigerator for up to 3 days and reheated in an oven or toaster oven at 325°F for 5 to 7 minutes.

Note: These can be made gluten free by substituting the all-purpose flour with almond flour using a 1:1 ratio.

Frituras de Maíz

Corn Fritters

Serves 6 to 8

vegetarian

What you'll need

2 cups canned or frozen corn kernels, thawed (not creamed corn)

1 garlic clove, minced

3 tablespoons minced sweet onion

3 large eggs, beaten

3 tablespoons whole milk

1 tablespoon sugar

1 teaspoon salt

1 teaspoon baking powder

½ teaspoon white pepper

½ teaspoon sweet or smoked paprika

4 to 5 tablespoons all-purpose flour

2 to 3 cups canola oil

What you'll do

Combine the corn, garlic, onion, eggs, milk, sugar, salt, baking powder, pepper, paprika, and 4 tablespoons of flour in a food processor or blender and blend well. Add the additional tablespoon of flour if the batter does not hold together on a tablespoon (it should be thick).

Heat about 2 inches of oil in a large frying pan over medium-high heat. Drop the batter by heaping tablespoons into the hot oil; the fritters should puff up a little. Fry for about 4 minutes, turning the fritters when the edges look golden, after about 2 minutes. Transfer the fritters to a paper towel–lined plate and serve immediately with cold beers all around.

Frituras de Malanga

Malanga Fritters

Serves 6 to 8

vegetarian

What you'll need

2 cups peeled and cubed malanga, boiled for 3 minutes

2 large eggs

1 garlic clove, minced

3 tablespoons minced sweet onion

1 teaspoon salt

½ teaspoon white pepper

½ teaspoon sweet or smoked paprika

2 tablespoons all-purpose flour

2 to 3 cups canola oil

What you'll do

Combine the malanga, eggs, garlic, onion, salt, pepper, paprika, and flour in a food processor or blender and blend well. The batter should be thick.

Heat about 2 inches of oil in a large frying pan over medium-high heat. Drop the batter by heaping tablespoons into the hot oil; the fritters should puff up a little. Fry for about 4 minutes, turning the fritters when the edges look golden, after about 2 minutes. Transfer the fritters to a paper towel–lined plate and serve immediately.

Green Plantain Hash

Fufú! With the accent on the second *u.* Isn't that the best word? I couldn't wait for the days my mom would make this dish just so I could hear her say it. I would ask her over and over again: "What's for dinner?" Then my brother would ask her, and we would ask my grandmother, and then my dad. I still think it's funny. But funny as it may sound, fufú has the most unique flavor and texture of almost any Cuban dish. *Fufú de plátano* is a great example of the West African influence on Caribbean food. It is a hearty and satisfying dish that is sure to become a family favorite.

gluten free

What you'll need

4 green plantains, peeled and cut into slices

⅓ cup olive oil

1 pound ham steak, cubed

1 medium onion, chopped

3 garlic cloves, minced

1 medium red bell pepper, chopped

½ teaspoon sweet or smoked paprika

½ teaspoon salt

½ teaspoon black pepper

What you'll do

Fill a large pot with water, add the plantain slices, and bring to a boil. Let the plantains boil for 40 to 45 minutes, until tender. Drain the plantains and set them aside.

Heat the olive oil in a large frying pan over medium-high heat. Add the ham and cook for about 3 minutes. Add the onion, garlic, and bell pepper and reduce the heat to medium. Cook for 5 to 7 minutes, until the onion is translucent.

Add the plantains and mash them into the onion-and-ham mixture with the back of a wooden spoon or a large fork. Add the paprika, salt, and pepper, and continue mashing and stirring. Taste and adjust the seasonings, if necessary. Serve immediately.

Fufú can be stored covered in the refrigerator for up to 3 days.

Note: Omit the ham for a vegetarian option.

vegetarian ALTERNATIVE

Fried Yuca

vegan

gluten free

The French (or Belgians, really) have French fries. The Cubans have *yuca frita*. And just as French fries taste great when dipped in ketchup, yuca frita taste best when dunked in garlic cilantro sauce. Actually, everything tastes better dunked in garlic cilantro sauce (recipe follows!).

What you'll need

1-pound bag frozen yuca

2 to 3 cups canola oil

Salt and pepper

What you'll do

Bring a large pot of salted water to a boil over high heat. Add the frozen yuca, then reduce the heat to low and simmer for 40 to 50 minutes, until the yuca is very tender.

Drain the yuca and cut it into large sticks the size of steak fries. Pat the yuca dry with paper towels to prevent the hot oil from splattering.

In a deep skillet (or use a deep fryer), preheat 3 inches of oil to 350°F. Fry the yuca in batches (do not crowd the pan) until light golden brown, turning once. This should take about 3 to 4 minutes. Drain on paper towel and sprinkle with salt immediately.

Serve with garlic cilantro dipping sauce.

Garlic Cilantro Dipping Sauce

keto friendly

vegetarian

gluten free

This makes a nice-sized batch and you'll literally want to dip everything in this addictive sauce. Keep in the refrigerator covered with a tight lid for 3 to 5 days.

What you'll need

1 bunch fresh cilantro, stems removed, leaves finely chopped

1½ cups mayonnaise (see Note)

¼ fresh cup minced garlic (about 6 to 8 cloves, depending on how garlicky you like it)

Salt and pepper

What you'll do

Combine the cilantro, mayonnaise, garlic, and salt and pepper to taste in a bowl. Mix until all of the ingredients are uniformly combined. You may add a tablespoon or two of water to thin out the sauce. Adjust salt and pepper as desired.

Note: Substitute vegan mayonnaise for traditional mayo to make the recipe vegan friendly.

vegan ALTERNA

Stuffed Green Plantains

pescatarian

gluten free

Tostones are perfectly delightful on their own, but when you stuff them, they are extra special. The number of things you can stuff them with is almost infinite. This recipe, which features a shrimp stuffing, is one of my favorites from the famed Versailles restaurant. But feel free to stuff yours with leftover *picadillo* or *Ropa Vieja* (recipe on page 88). In Miami, the Toston burger is quite popular. And yes, it is exactly what you would think. A burger with all the fixings between two crispy on the outside, tender on the inside, perfectly fried tostones. What's not to love?

What you'll need

6 slices canned pineapple

4 tablespoons olive oil

½ cup finely diced onion

¼ cup finely diced green bell pepper

2 garlic cloves, finely minced

¾ cup crushed tomatoes

¼ teaspoon crushed red pepper

Pinch of ground cumin

¼ cup *vino seco* (dry cooking wine)

Salt and pepper

1 pound medium shrimp, peeled and deveined

Approximately 12 to 16 freshly fried *tostones* (page 125)

¼ cup fresh cilantro, finely chopped

What you'll do

Place the pineapple slices in a hot nonstick pan and cook over medium-high heat until golden brown, about 3 minutes per side. Cut into ½-inch pieces and set aside.

Heat 3 tablespoons of the oil in the same skillet over medium-high heat and add the onion and bell pepper. Cook for about 3 minutes, stirring occasionally, and add the garlic. Continue cooking for another 3 minutes, stirring frequently to make sure the garlic doesn't burn.

Add the tomatoes, crushed red pepper, and cumin and continue cooking for an additional 7 to 8 minutes. Add the cooking wine and salt and pepper to taste and continue cooking for an additional 3 minutes. Remove from heat and set aside.

In a separate skillet, heat the remaining tablespoon of oil over medium-high heat. Season the shrimp with salt and pepper. Add the shrimp and reserved pineapple and cook, stirring frequently, until the shrimp are opaque, 2 to 3 minutes.

Add the shrimp and pineapple to the tomato mixture and continue cooking for 2 or 3 minutes more, until the shrimp are opaque. Adjust seasoning if necessary. Top the freshly fried *tostones* with 1 to 1½ tablespoons of the shrimp mixture, depending on the size of the *toston*. Garnish with chopped cilantro and serve immediately.

Fried Pork Chunks

Is there anything better or more representative of Cuban cuisine than fried pork? Probably not. After all, it is the marriage of two of our favorite things: pork and frying. The pork shoulder can be cubed large for an entrée, but I love to make small cubes and serve them with a bunch of other small plates and some of my Skinny Latina hot sauce on the side.

keto friendly

gluten free

What you'll need

2 pounds pork shoulder, cut into 2-inch cubes

1 cup mojo (page 11)

1½ cups water salted with 1 teaspoon salt

¼ cup vegetable oil

Slices of raw onion and lime wedges, for serving

Serve with additional mojo or garlic cilantro sauce (page 28)

What you'll do

Marinate the pork cubes in the mojo for a minimum of 4 hours or overnight.

Remove the pork from the marinade and pat dry.

In a heavy-bottomed pot, bring the salted water, vegetable oil, and marinated pork chunks to a boil. Allow to boil uncovered for 3 minutes. Reduce the heat to low and continue cooking uncovered, stirring occasionally, until all the water evaporates, about 35–45 minutes.

Brown the pork chunks in the rendered fat in the bottom of the pot until golden and crispy on the outside. Toss in the raw onions and remove from heat. Serve with extra mojo and lime wedges.

Spanish Omelet

gluten free

Spain's influence on Cuban food is undeniable. This *tortilla* is proof. Often served as an appetizer, it can be eaten hot or at room temperature. Brimming with potatoes, chorizo, and onions, it is a meal in itself, and cut into wedges, it's the perfect appetizer.

What you'll need

2 to 3 cups vegetable oil

2 large potatoes, peeled and cut into ½-inch cubes

¼ cup olive oil

¾ pound Spanish chorizo sausage, roughly chopped

1 medium onion, roughly chopped

6 large eggs

1 teaspoon salt

½ teaspoon black pepper

What you'll do

Heat about 2 inches of vegetable oil in a large frying pan over medium-high heat. Carefully place the potatoes in the oil in a single layer and reduce heat to medium. Fry the potatoes for 5 to 7 minutes, until they are a light golden brown. Transfer the cooked potatoes to a paper towel to drain and cool to room temperature. (You also can use leftover cooked potatoes in this; just be sure they are at room temperature before adding them to the omelet.)

Heat the olive oil in a medium nonstick frying pan over medium heat. Add the chorizo and onion and sauté for 5 to 7 minutes, until the onion is translucent. Add the potatoes, spreading them out evenly so they cover the bottom of the pan and are evenly distributed among the rest of the ingredients.

Crack the eggs into a large bowl, add the salt and pepper, and mix thoroughly with a fork. Pour the eggs evenly over the potato–chorizo mixture. Allow the omelet to cook, undisturbed, for 5 to 7 minutes, until the bottom of the omelet is golden brown and set.

Slide the omelet carefully onto a plate (preferably one that is larger than the pan), flip the pan over the plate, then quickly invert them both, so the uncooked side of the omelet ends up face-down in the pan. Cook for 4 to 5 minutes. Slide the omelet onto a plate, cut it into wedges, and serve immediately.

TRES

SOUPS AND STEWS FOR THE HEART AND SOUL

Soups are an integral part of Cuban cuisine. They are the foundation of every meal, providing heartiness and warmth, the two most important aspects of any Cuban meal. But don't think that these soups are the watery, overly salted soups that many of us are, unfortunately, used to. I mean, when you think of soup, don't you envision some type of broth-like substance? Well, these soups are nothing like that; they are thick and substantial. In fact, many of them include beans and rice and, of course, savory *sofrito*, the heart of Cuban cuisine.

Almost every childhood meal I remember involved beans or legumes of some kind. I would often wake up to the wonderful aromas of soup—be it black bean, red bean, split pea, lentil, or a variety of others. It wasn't so much the aromas that woke me, but the soothing sound that only a pressure cooker can make. Many Cuban moms and grandmas began cooking early in the day, usually starting with beans. It's a habit that began back in Cuba, when husbands came home from work at lunchtime for a little, you know, soup. Cuban soups and stews are hearty and also nutritious. They're the best introduction to "modern Cuban" cooking because most can be adapted to satisfy everyone's preferences or dietary needs.

Black Bean Soup

vegan

gluten free

You will find a recipe for black bean soup in every Cuban cookbook. It's mandatory. I'm not kidding; I actually think there is some kind of publishing law that requires it. But don't be fooled—not all black beans are created equal. While I'd love to tell you that mine are the absolute best—well, they *are*—I suppose there may be some other marginally good recipes out there. What is certain is that black beans are considered the food of the gods by most Cubans. One taste of this recipe, and you'll see why.

Soaking your beans overnight before you cook them makes the cooking process much quicker and produces beans that are uniformly tender.

What you'll need

1 pound dry black beans, picked through and rinsed

¼ cup olive oil

1 large onion, chopped

3 garlic cloves, minced

1 green bell pepper, chopped

2 tablespoons tomato paste

1 bay leaf

½ teaspoon ground cumin

½ teaspoon dried oregano leaves

2 tablespoons red wine vinegar

2 tablespoons sugar

1 cup *vino seco* (dry white cooking wine)

Salt and pepper

6 to 8 cups *Arroz Blanco* (White Rice; page 70), for serving

What you'll do

Place the beans in a large bowl and add enough room temperature water to cover. Soak the beans for at least 6 hours, preferably overnight. (If you are soaking them for just 6 hours, use slightly warm or tepid water instead.)

Drain the beans and set them aside.

Heat the olive oil in a large stockpot over medium heat. Add the onion, garlic, and bell pepper and sauté for 5 to 7 minutes, until the vegetables soften. Add the tomato paste, bay leaf, cumin, and oregano and stir well. Add the beans and 1½ quarts water and bring to a boil.

Let the soup boil for about 10 minutes, then reduce the heat to low. Add the vinegar, sugar, and *vino seco,* and stir well. Cover the pot and let the soup simmer for 3 to 3½ hours, until the beans are soft and tender and the stock has thickened. (The stock will thicken as the beans cool to room temperature.) Remove and discard the bay leaf. Season the soup generously with salt and a sprinkling of pepper. Serve over the long-grain white rice.

Store the beans in an airtight container in the refrigerator for 3 to 5 days. Freeze cooled beans for up to 2 months.

Red Bean Soup

Another favorite of Cuban cuisine is red bean soup or *frijoles colorados*. These beans are a bit different from the ever-popular black beans. Here, the tomato base and chorizo impart a tangy and unique flavor to the beans. The addition of vegetables makes this a perfect one-dish meal: hearty and delicious.

   Make sure you don't confuse these small, oval, red beans with kidney beans. And remember: Soaking the beans overnight helps them cook more quickly and evenly. This soup may be served alone or over fluffy white rice.

What you'll need

1 pound dry red beans

¼ cup olive oil

1 large onion, diced

3 garlic cloves, minced

1 medium green bell pepper, chopped

8 ounces Spanish chorizo sausage

4 ounces ham hock, optional

1 bay leaf

½ cup canned tomato sauce

1 cup peeled and diced red-skinned potatoes

1 cup chopped *calabaza* (a pumpkinlike squash)

1 cup *vino seco* (dry white cooking wine)

Salt and pepper

Arroz Blanco (White Rice; page 70), for serving

What you'll do

Place the beans in a large bowl and add enough room temperature water to cover. Soak the beans for at least 6 hours, preferably overnight. (If you are soaking them for just 6 hours, use slightly warm or tepid water instead.)

Drain the beans and set them aside.

Heat the olive oil in a large stockpot over medium heat. Add the onion, garlic, and bell pepper and sauté for 5 to 7 minutes, until the vegetables soften.

Add the chorizo (I remove the casing before adding it, but it is not necessary) and the ham hock, then cook for 5 to 7 minutes to render some of the fat from the meat.

Reduce the heat to low and add the bay leaf and tomato sauce. Continue cooking over low heat for another 5 minutes.

Add 1½ quarts water and the *vino seco,* then raise the heat to high. Bring the soup to a boil, stirring frequently. Let the soup boil for 10 minutes.

Reduce the heat to low, cover the pot, and cook the soup for 2 to 2½ hours, until it thickens slightly. Remove the bay leaf, chorizo, and ham hock. Cut the chorizo into ½-inch slices and return them to the pot. Discard the bay leaf and ham hock.

Add the potatoes and the *calabaza,* then bring the soup to a boil. Reduce the heat to low and cover. Continue cooking over low heat until the vegetables are fork-tender. Add salt and pepper to taste. This soup may be served alone or over fluffy white rice.

Note: This recipe can easily be made vegan or vegetarian by substituting vegetable stock and omitting the animal protein with excellent results.

vegan/
vegetarian
ALTERNATIVE

Plantain Soup

vegan

gluten free

If you were stranded on a deserted island with nothing but plantains and, say, this book, you certainly would have no shortage of recipes. This soup is creamy and satisfying. It is also surprisingly easy to make. Don't forget to garnish with some crispy plantain chips.

What you'll need

¼ cup olive oil

1 medium onion, diced

2 garlic cloves, minced

½ cup diced carrot

¼ cup diced celery

6 cups low-sodium beef stock

3 green plantains, peeled and diced

1 bay leaf

1 teaspoon salt

½ teaspoon ground cumin

½ teaspoon ground coriander

½ teaspoon black pepper

½ teaspoon sweet or smoked paprika

3 tablespoons fresh lime juice
(1½ to 2 limes)

Mariquitas (Plantain Chips; page 16),
for garnish

What you'll do

Heat the olive oil in a large, heavy pot over medium heat. Add the onion and garlic, and sauté for 5 minutes, until they both soften slightly.

Add the carrot and celery, and cook for another 5 minutes, stirring frequently. Add the remaining ingredients, raise the heat to high, and bring the soup to a rapid boil. Boil for 3 minutes, stirring frequently.

Reduce the heat to low, cover the pot, and simmer for 35 to 40 minutes, until the plantains are tender. Remove the pot from the heat and allow the soup to cool a bit. Remove and discard the bay leaf.

Using an immersion blender or working in small batches with a standard blender or food processor, purée the soup until it is creamy. Taste the soup and adjust the seasonings, if necessary. Serve hot, garnished with the *mariquitas.*

Sopa de Pollo

Cuban-Style Chicken Soup

Serves 6 to 8

The only time I recall having soup as a full meal was when I was sick. The second my mother thought I had *destemplanza* (a mysterious Cuban malady, wherein your body temperature is one degree higher than normal, greatly increasing the probability of imminent death from pneumonia), she would begin a pot of chicken soup (also known as Cuban penicillin). Cuban chicken soup is by far the best chicken soup you'll ever taste.

In this recipe, I suggest using chicken breasts, but you can use dark meat or a combination of white and dark, if you prefer. *Malanga* is a root vegetable found in most Hispanic markets. If you can't find it, you can use potatoes instead.

What you'll need

4 bone-in chicken breast halves, skin removed

1 garlic clove

1 bay leaf

1 teaspoon salt, plus more as needed

1 tablespoon tomato paste

2 tablespoons olive oil

1 medium onion, diced

2 celery stalks, diced

1 carrot, diced

1 cup chopped *calabaza* (pumpkinlike squash)

1 cup chopped *malanga*

4 ounces *fideos* or angel hair pasta

Salt and pepper

Lime wedge, for serving

What you'll do

Bring 2 quarts of water to a boil in a large pot.

Add the chicken breasts, garlic, bay leaf, and salt. Reduce the heat to low, cover the pot, and simmer for at least 1 hour, until the chicken is cooked through and opaque. Transfer the chicken to a plate and set aside. Discard the garlic and bay leaf. Transfer the stock to another container and allow it to cool completely.

In a small cup, dissolve the tomato paste in ½ cup of the hot stock. Set aside.

Heat the olive oil in the same pot used to make the stock. Add the onion, celery, and carrot and sauté for about 5 minutes, until the onion is soft and translucent. Add the *calabaza, malanga,* the tomato paste mixture, and the stock. The stock should cover the vegetables by 3 to 4 inches. If the stock is too low, add more water.

Bring the soup to a boil, then reduce the heat to low, cover the pot, and let the soup simmer until the vegetables are soft and tender, about 40 minutes.

Remove the chicken from the bone and tear it into pieces with your hands. (I prefer this method to chopping it with a knife because the chicken retains more moisture and flavor.) Add the chicken and the *fideos* to the stock and stir to incorporate. Bring the soup to a boil again, then immediately turn off the heat and season the soup with salt and pepper to taste. Stir well and add a squeeze of lime before serving.

Meat and Vegetable Stew

Serves 8 to 10

Ok, let me be perfectly honest: I never ate *ajiaco,* this hearty meat and vegetable stew, until I was well into my adult years. It isn't because it's not good. In fact, most Cubans love it (apparently, it's Cuba's national dish). As a child, I just didn't like the name, which, when pronounced correctly, sounds like *Ah-jee-you-ko.* I'll admit it, to me, it doesn't sound very appetizing. In fact, when we were growing up, my brother and I used to call it "yuck soup" because the name reminded us of the word "yuck."

But, since this book is about traditional Cuban cuisine, and it is actually delicious and satisfying, here it is. My mom's recipe for yuck soup, I mean *ajiaco.*

What you'll need

½-pound *tasajo* (salt-cured beef)

1 pound flank steak

1½ pounds pork loin, cut into 1-inch chunks

1 bay leaf

1 *malanga,* peeled and cut into 1½-inch cubes

1 *boniato,* peeled and cut into 1½-inch cubes

1 yuca, cut into 1½-inch cubes

1 green plantain, peeled and cut crosswise into 2-inch-thick slices

1 sweet (black) plantain, peeled and cut crosswise into 1-inch-thick slices

1 (¾-pound) *calabaza* (a pumpkinlike squash), peeled and cut into 1½-inch cubes

3 ears corn, cut into 2-inch-thick slices

½ cup olive oil

4 garlic cloves, chopped

1 medium green bell pepper, chopped

2 medium onions, chopped

1 cup canned tomato sauce

½ teaspoon dried oregano leaves

½ teaspoon ground cumin

1 to 2 teaspoons salt

½ teaspoon white pepper

What you'll do

Place the *tasajo* in a bowl and add lukewarm water to cover. Soak for about 2 hours, changing the water every 30 minutes. Rinse and set aside.

Bring 3 quarts of water to a boil in a large stockpot over high heat. Add the *tasajo,* flank steak, pork, and bay leaf. Reduce the heat to medium-low and simmer for 1½ hours—the broth will reduce by at least one-third. Skim the top of the stock occasionally to remove any residue.

Add the *malanga, boniato,* yuca, green plantain, sweet plantain, *calabaza,* and corn, stirring to incorporate each vegetable before adding the next. Cover the pot, raise the heat to medium, and continue cooking until all the vegetables are cooked through, 25 to 30 minutes.

Heat the olive oil in a pan over medium-high heat. Add the garlic, bell pepper, and onion, and sauté for 5 to 7 minutes, until the vegetables soften and the flavors are well incorporated. Add the tomato sauce and lower the heat. Simmer for 20 minutes. This is your *sofrito,* an essential Cuban addition.

Add the *sofrito* to the stockpot and stir well. Stir in the oregano, cumin, salt, and black pepper. Remove and discard the bay leaf.

Country-Style Lentil Soup

Lentil soup is a Cuban favorite because it is so hearty and nutritious. In our attempts to Americanize everything, we call this lentil soup *campesina* or "country style." We believe that because we add some carrots and taters to a dish, we should be out steering cattle. Of course, we also add ham, chorizo, and *calabaza;* not exactly what one would call "home on the range," but good, nonetheless.

What you'll need

¼ cup olive oil

¼ pound cooking ham, diced

¼ pound Spanish chorizo sausage, diced

3 garlic cloves, minced

1 large onion, diced

6 cups homemade or low-sodium canned chicken stock

½ cup canned tomato sauce

¼ cup *vino seco* (dry white cooking wine)

1 tablespoon red wine vinegar

1 pound dried lentils, rinsed in cold water and soaked for 30 minutes

2 large white potatoes, peeled and cut into 1-inch cubes

3 carrots, peeled and cut into ½-inch cubes

½ cup diced *calabaza* or pumpkin

1 bay leaf

½ teaspoon ground cumin

½ teaspoon sweet or smoked paprika

½ teaspoon ground oregano

½ teaspoon salt

½ teaspoon black pepper

What you'll do

Heat 2 tablespoons of the olive oil in a large stockpot over medium heat. Add the ham and chorizo and sauté for 3 to 5 minutes, until the chorizo browns slightly. Add the garlic and onion and cook for another 5 minutes, until the onion softens.

Add the remaining ingredients, including another 2 tablespoons olive oil, and stir well. Bring the soup to a boil over medium heat and continue boiling for 5 minutes. Reduce the heat to low, cover the pot, and continue cooking, stirring occasionally, for 45 minutes to 1 hour, until the vegetables and lentils are tender. Taste and adjust the seasonings as necessary. Remove and discard the bay leaf.

Note: This recipe can easily be made vegan or vegetarian by substituting vegetable stock for the chicken stock and omitting the animal protein with excellent results.

vegan/
vegetarian
ALTERNATIVE

Soft Polenta with Pork

Tamales are a popular snack and party food among Cubans. They are often sold wrapped in the cornhusks in which they were boiled. In my neighborhood, you could either make *tamales* yourself or order smaller *tamales* wrapped in tiny foil packets from your local Cuban bakery. When I was a little girl, we always had *tamales* at my birthday parties. My mom used to spend hours making them.

Tamal en Cazuela is basically *tamales* in a pot—a creamy, thick, cornmeal-based soup that is delicious and satisfying. It is really the Cuban version of polenta. And since we Cubans need to add animal protein to *everything,* this recipe includes pork (of course). Be sure to marinate the pork for at least 30 minutes and up to 24 hours.

What you'll need

½ cup fresh sour orange juice or a mixture of equal parts lime juice and orange juice

4 teaspoons salt

1 teaspoon white pepper

½ teaspoon sweet or smoked paprika

½ teaspoon ground cumin

1 pound lean pork loin, cut into 1-inch chunks

⅓ cup olive oil

1 small green bell pepper, chopped

1 large onion, chopped

4 garlic cloves, minced

1½ cups canned tomato sauce

½ cup *vino seco* (dry white cooking wine) or dry sherry

1 bay leaf

12 ounces Spanish chorizo sausage, coarsely chopped

1½ cups yellow cornmeal

2 teaspoons red wine vinegar

Hot sauce and lime wedges, for serving

What you'll do

Combine the sour orange juice, 2 teaspoons of the salt, ½ teaspoon of the black pepper, the paprika, and cumin in a large, nonreactive bowl. Add the pork, cover the bowl with plastic wrap, and let the pork marinate for at least 30 minutes, or up to 24 hours. (Refrigerate it if you plan on marinating it longer than 1 hour.)

Heat 2 tablespoons of the olive oil in a sauté pan over medium heat. Add the bell pepper, onion, and garlic, and sauté for 5 to 7 minutes, until the vegetables soften. Add the tomato sauce, *vino seco,* bay leaf, and wine, then bring to a boil. Add the chorizo, reduce the heat to low, cover the pan, and simmer for 15 to 20 minutes, allowing the wine to evaporate, the flavors to deepen, and the tomato sauce to cook down a bit. Set aside.

Drain the marinade from the pork.

In a separate frying pan, heat 2 to 3 tablespoons of the olive oil (depending on how lean your meat is) over medium-high heat. Add the pork and sear the pieces on all sides, about 4 to 6 minutes or until golden. Reduce the heat to medium and cook for another 5 minutes. Set aside.

In a large stockpot, bring 2 quarts water to a boil. Add the remaining 2 teaspoons salt, ½ teaspoon pepper, and the remaining olive oil. Add the cornmeal, stirring continuously with a wire whisk. Reduce the heat to low and continue cooking, stirring occasionally, for 30 to 45 minutes, until the mixture thickens and becomes creamy.

Add the chorizo mixture and stir well. Taste and adjust the seasonings, if necessary. Remove and discard the bay leaf.

To serve, top a steaming bowl of this dense, creamy soup with the crispy pork chunks. Season with hot sauce and a squeeze of lime.

Note: I've made this recipe for vegetarian or vegan friends by using vegetable stock and substituting picadillo made with ground walnuts or Impossible ground beef for the pork. It is always a hit.

Polenta with Crabmeat   Serves 6

Harina is traditional Cuban comfort food. It's really a simple polenta that, over the years, has become quite popular among the foodie set. But Cubans have been making this forever—as baby food, or as simple peasant food with a fried egg on top. Not exactly gourmet, right? But with the addition of savory sofrito-infused crabmeat, it's a whole different story.

What you'll need

For the Crab

¼ cup olive oil

1 cup chopped onion

3 garlic cloves, minced

½ cup chopped green bell pepper

1 cup canned tomato sauce

¼ cup *vino seco* (dry white cooking wine)

¼ cup diced pimentos

1 bay leaf

Tabasco or other hot sauce, optional

1 teaspoon salt

½ teaspoon black pepper

½ teaspoon sweet or smoked paprika

1 pound fresh lump crabmeat, picked clean

For the Harina

1½ cups fine-ground yellow cornmeal

3 tablespoons olive oil

1 teaspoon salt

½ teaspoon white ground pepper

½ teaspoon sweet or smoked paprika

What you'll do

To make the crab: Heat the olive oil in a large frying pan over medium heat. Add the onion, garlic, and bell pepper, and sauté for 5 to 7 minutes, until the vegetables are tender. Add the tomato sauce, *vino seco,* pimentos, bay leaf, Tabasco, salt, black pepper, and paprika, and cook for 5 minutes. Stir in the crabmeat and taste to adjust the seasonings, if necessary. Set aside.

To make the *harina:* Bring 2 quarts water to a boil in a large pot. Add the cornmeal, olive oil, salt, white pepper, and paprika, stirring frequently with a wire whisk. Reduce the heat to low, cover the pot, and cook for another 35 to 40 minutes, until the *harina* is thick and creamy, stirring occasionally to prevent lumps from forming. Taste the *harina* and adjust the seasonings, if necessary.

To serve, spoon the *harina* into deep bowls and top with the tomato-crab mixture.

Asturian Bean Stew

Every self-respecting Cuban loves *Fabada,* this rich bean stew that is a close cousin to the classic French *cassoulet.* Few, however, venture to make it themselves. It's actually much easier than you might think. All you need to set the scene is a cold night (rare in Miami), a bunch of friends, and a big pitcher of sangria. Obviously, you'll need the ingredients, too.

Some of the ingredients in this stew are quite unique and may be difficult to find. I have substituted cannellini beans for the *fabas* many times with excellent results. The blood sausage and ham hocks are optional, and I often leave them out or substitute diced ham steak and Spanish chorizo.

What you'll need

2 tablespoons olive oil

1 small white onion, finely sliced

2 garlic cloves, minced

¾ pound Spanish chorizo sausage

4 pounds *jamón Serrano* (Serrano ham)

½ pound *lacón* or ham hocks, optional

1 pound *fabas,* rinsed, soaked overnight, and drained

1 pound *morcilla,* optional

1 teaspoon sweet or smoked paprika

3 or 4 saffron threads

Salt and pepper

Chopped fresh flat-leaf parsley, for garnish

Pan Frito (Fried Cuban Bread; page 23), for serving

What you'll do

Heat the olive oil in a large, heavy pot over medium heat. Add the onion and garlic, and sauté for 5 to 7 minutes, until the onions are translucent. Add the chorizo, ham, *lacón,* and *morcilla,* and stir well. Cook for 5 minutes. Add the beans and enough water to cover, then bring to a gentle boil. Reduce the temperature to low, cover the pot, and let the soup simmer for about 1½ hours, stirring occasionally, until the beans are tender. If necessary, add additional water to keep the beans and meat covered.

Remove from the heat and cool to room temperature to allow the flavors and textures of the soup to develop. Taste and adjust the seasonings, if necessary.

Reheat the soup before serving. Garnish with parsley and a drizzle of olive oil and serve with *pan frito.*

Store in the refrigerator in an airtight container for up to 3 days.

Caldo Gallego

Galician Bean Soup

Caldo gallego is a substantial and scrumptious white bean soup that originated in Galicia, Spain, and has since been usurped by Cubans and added to their cuisine. I love it because it is the perfect excuse to make a big of batch of *Pan Frito* (Fried Cuban Bread; page 23)—the soup being the perfect accompaniment to the bread, of course.

What you'll need

1 pound dry white beans (such as navy, kidney, or great northern), rinsed, soaked overnight, and drained

½ pound ham hock or shank bones

½ pound flank steak

3 ounces cured pork fatback or salt pork, rind removed

1 small turnip, halved

1 large onion, diced

3 garlic cloves, minced

3 medium potatoes, diced

½ pound Spanish chorizo sausage, sliced

Salt and pepper

2 cups chopped collard greens or turnip greens

3 tablespoons olive oil

1 recipe *Pan Frito* (Fried Cuban Bread; page 23), for serving

What you'll do

Combine 2 quarts water, the beans, ham hock, flank steak, pork fatback, turnip, onion, and garlic in a large pot over medium-high heat. Bring the soup to a boil; boil for 10 minutes. Reduce the heat to low, cover the pot, and cook the soup for 2 to 2½ hours.

Remove the soup from the heat and let it sit for 15 to 30 minutes, so the soup can thicken and the flavors come together. Remove the ham hock, fatback, turnip, and flank steak from the pot, discarding the fatback and turnip. Shred the flank steak and return it to the soup. Remove the meat from the ham hock and return it to the soup. Discard the bones.

Add the potatoes, chorizo, and salt and pepper to taste. Cover the pot and let the soup cook over low heat for another 30 to 45 minutes, until the potatoes are fork-tender. During the last 10 minutes of the cooking process, add the collard greens and olive oil. Taste the soup and adjust the seasonings, if necessary. Serve piping hot with the *pan frito*.

CUATRO

SATISFYING SANDWICHES
AND SALADS

Cuban sandwiches are also unlike their American counterparts.
In fact, the word "sandwich" doesn't really do these sandwich
recipes justice. While you might envision two pieces of Wonder
Bread slapped together with cheese or meat between the slices
and maybe some unfortunate-looking pieces of lettuce, these
sandwiches are a far cry from your typical "turkey on whole wheat,
hold the mayo."

Pretty much everyone has heard of the Cuban Sandwich, or
Sanguiche Cubano, as it's referred to in most Cuban establishments.
If you haven't, you must make one of these immediately. They are
simply irresistible. *Pan con Bistec,* or Steak Sandwich, is also a popular item that is equally delectable. In addition to these fine recipes,
I show you how to make other traditional Cuban favorites, like the
Frita (Cuban-Style Hamburger), *Medianoche* (Midnight Sandwich),
and *Croqueta Preparada* (Croquette Sandwich). So, prepare yourself
for a unique sandwich experience—a festival of flavors, and the
kind of satisfaction you could never get from tuna on rye.

Cuban salads are akin to all other types of Cuban cuisine—
wholesome and filling. You won't hear a Cuban woman claim to be
starving, then order something like, "Endive salad, no dressing."
Our salads are in *addition to* a good Cuban meal. I wholeheartedly
recommend any of the salad recipes in this chapter.

Cuban Sandwich

A meal in itself, the Cuban sandwich is hearty and delicious. It is best to use a sandwich press to make it. In a pinch, you can use a waffle iron or even weigh it down with a foil paper–covered brick or a heavy cast iron skillet.

This recipe makes two HUGE sandwiches or four "normal" sandwiches. I am not going to dictate exact portions here.

What you'll need

1 (2-foot) loaf Cuban bread

Mayonnaise

Mustard

About ½ Swiss cheese, thinly sliced

About ½ pound sweet ham, thinly sliced

About ½ pound lean pork, thinly sliced

Thin dill pickles slices

Salted butter, at room temperature

What you'll do

Preheat a large frying pan or cast iron skillet over medium-low heat or a sandwich press to 300°F.

Cut the loaf of bread in half, horizontally. Remove a little of the bread from the inside of one half of the bread.

Combine equal parts mayo and mustard (I prefer Dijon) in a bowl and spread the mixture evenly on both sides of the bread. Layer half the cheese on the bottom half of the bread, followed by the ham and pork. Layer pickles on top of the pork, then the other half of the cheese. Top with the top half of the bread, then press the sandwich down a little.

Cut the sandwich into desired portions and brush the outside crusts with butter. Place the sandwich on the preheated pan or sandwich press and press down on the sandwich with the top of the sandwich press or a heavy cast iron pan. Cook for about 5 minutes, until the sandwich is heated through and the cheese is melted.

Variation: *Croqueta Preparada*

Croquette Sandwich

The famous *croqueta preparada* is simply a Cuban sandwich with three or four freshly fried ham croquetas placed between the cheese and the ham and pork before pressing down. For Ham Croquetas recipe, see page 20.

Midnight Sandwich

A *medianoche,* or midnight sandwich, is very similar to a Cuban sandwich. The only real difference is the bread that is used to make it. A *medianoche,* so named because it was usually enjoyed after a long night of clubbing, is made using a soft eggy roll that is a little sweet and long like a hoagie. Hispanic markets or Cuban bakeries carry them. At regular supermarkets, look for a long egg roll (think hot dog bun, but wider) that is a little shiny on top.

What you'll need

1 (6-inch) *medianoche* roll or other sweet, eggy roll

Mayonnaise

Mustard

2 to 4 slices dill pickles

4 slices Swiss cheese

4 slices sweet ham

4 thin slices roast pork

Salted butter, at room temperature

What you'll do

Preheat a large frying pan over medium-low heat or a sandwich press to 300°F.

Cut the roll in half horizontally and spread mayonnaise on one half and mustard on the other. Arrange the pickles across the bottom half of the bread and top with 2 slices of Swiss cheese. Layer the ham, pork, remaining 2 slices of cheese, and the top half of the bread.

Brush the outside of the sandwich with butter, then place it on the sandwich press or preheated skillet and press down with the top of the sandwich press or a heavy cast iron pan. Cook for 5 to 7 minutes, until the sandwich is heated through and the cheese is melted.

Steak Sandwich

Pan con bistec appears on the menu at almost every Cuban restaurant. Ironically, I've seen a lot of variations on how it is made. This is my favorite, with just the steak, sautéed onions, and fried potato sticks; a little ketchup and hot sauce finishes it off perfectly.

What you'll need

2 tablespoons olive oil

½ cup sliced onion

Top round or sirloin steak, pounded to ¼ inch thick, or 1 *palomilla* or minute steak

Garlic powder

Salt

1 (2-foot) loaf Cuban bread, split horizontally

Papitas Fritas (French Fried Potatoes; page 121)

Ketchup

Shredded lettuce

Sliced tomatoes

What you'll do

Heat the olive oil in a cast iron skillet over medium-high heat. Add the onion and sauté for 5 to 7 minutes, until soft. Transfer the onion to a plate and reheat the skillet over medium-high.

Season the steak generously with garlic powder and salt. Add it to the hot skillet and fry it for 1 to 2 minutes per side, until it is cooked to the desired doneness.

Place the steak on the bottom half of the bread and top with the sautéed onions and any pan drippings. Top with a mound of crispy fries, ketchup, lettuce, tomatoes, and the other half of the bread.

Cuban Hamburgers

Fritas, the Cuban equivalent of hamburgers, creates the same effect as Krispy Kreme dough-nuts—you can't eat just one. This recipe calls for ground chorizo. While some Hispanic markets sell chorizo already ground, you can easily make this by removing the casings, cutting the chorizo into small pieces, and blitzing the meat in a food processor. Make sure the chorizo is at room temperature before you do this; it just makes the whole process easier.

What you'll need

¼ cup half-and-half or evaporated milk

¼ cup fresh white bread crumbs

1½ teaspoon *pimentón dulce* or sweet paprika

2 tablespoons Worcestershire sauce

2 tablespoons chili sauce or ketchup

1 large egg, beaten

1 pound lean ground beef

½ pound ground Spanish chorizo sausage

½ teaspoon salt

½ teaspoon black pepper

3 tablespoons olive oil

10 to 12 small, round potato rolls or soft dinner rolls, warmed

Ketchup

Mayonnaise

Papitas Fritas (French Fried Potatoes; page 121)

What you'll do

Combine the half-and-half, bread crumbs, *pimentón dulce,* Worcestershire sauce, and chili sauce in a bowl. Add the egg and stir to incorporate.

In another bowl, combine the beef, chorizo, salt, and pepper. Add the half-and-half mixture and combine by lightly kneading the ingredients with your hands.

Divide the meat into 10 or 12 equal-sized balls; flatten each to about ½ inch thick.

Heat the oil in a cast iron skillet over medium-high heat. Add the meat patties and fry for 5 to 7 minutes per side, until the burgers are cooked to your desired doneness.

Place each burger inside a soft warm roll and top each patty with a little ketchup and mayonnaise.

Serve with a *ton* of thin, crispy fries. Then eat just one *frita.*

Just kidding!

> Note: For a vegetarian option, you may substitute a mixture of Impossible meat and Impossible ground sausage for the beef and chorizo in this recipe. Add an extra tablespoon of smoked paprika to the mix to give the burgers that great smoky flavor.

vegetarian
ALTERNATIVE

I've often wondered about this Elena Ruz person. Who was she? Why was a sandwich named after her? I did a little digging and it turns out that she was a real person who lived in Cuba. She would frequent a restaurant called El Caramelo where she requested that her sandwich be made in this particular way so often, they put it on the menu and named it after her. It's become very popular and can be found on the menu at most Cuban restaurants and sandwich shops.

What you'll need

1 ounce cream cheese, at room temperature

2 slices white bread

1 tablespoon strawberry preserves

3 ounces shaved turkey breast

What you'll do

Preheat a sandwich grill or toaster oven to 350°F.

Spread the cream cheese on one slice of bread and the strawberry preserves on the other. Layer the turkey slices in between.

Place the sandwich in the sandwich press or wrap it in foil and heat it in the toaster oven for 3 to 5 minutes, until heated through.

Cuban Club Sandwich

Makes 2 big sandwiches or 4 "normal"-sized sandwiches.

I'm not going to lie; this sandwich didn't exist in Cuba and it is a pretty blatant attempt to copy the classic American club sandwich. Basically, we put a club sandwich on Cuban bread and voilà! The Calle Ocho sandwich was born. The sandwich is very popular so I had to include it. If you ask me, a club sandwich on Cuban bread is genius.

What you'll need

1 (2-foot) loaf Cuban bread

Mayonnaise

Mustard (I prefer Dijon)

About ½ pound Swiss cheese, thinly sliced

About ½ pound sweet ham, thinly sliced

About ½ pound turkey breast, thinly sliced

8 slices bacon, cooked until crispy

Thinly sliced tomatoes

Shredded lettuce

Salted butter, at room temperature

What you'll do

Preheat a large frying pan over medium-low heat or a sandwich press to 300°F. Cut the loaf of bread in half, horizontally. Remove a little of the bread on the inside of one half of the bread.

Combine equal parts mayo and mustard in a bowl and spread the mixture evenly on both sides of the bread. Layer half the cheese on the bottom half of the bread followed by the ham and turkey. Layer the bacon on top of the turkey, then the tomato. Top with the shredded lettuce, the remaining half of the cheese, and the top half of the bread.

Press the sandwich down a little. Cut the sandwich into the desired portions and brush the outside of each sandwich with butter.

Place the sandwiches on the grill and press down on the sandwiches with the top of the sandwich grill or a cast iron pan. Cook for about 5 minutes, until the sandwiches are heated through and the cheese is melted.

Roast Pork Sandwich

Pan con lechón was invented because Cubans never know what to do with leftover pork. You see, Cubans love to roast whole pigs. It's a kind of "prove your manhood" thing, so it is done often. The day after one particular pork fest, people bought loaves of Cuban bread, made *mojo criollo* (garlic sauce), and voilà! The *pan con lechón* was born! These sandwiches are so good, you no longer need to roast a whole pig to get one. You can order one anywhere, although they are still best when made with leftover roast pig.

What you'll need

1 (2-foot) loaf Cuban bread, cut in half horizontally, but not all the way through to the other side

¼ cup Mojo Criollo (page 11)

½- to ¾-pound roast pork, heated

Thinly sliced onion

What you'll do

Place the bread in a warm oven for a few minutes just to heat it through (not toast it).

Spread mojo on each side of the bread. Add the pork, then the onion, and the top half of the bread. Serve immediately.

Ensalada Cubana

Cuban Chopped Salad

Noche Buena at my house is a friends and family affair. Many of my daughters' friends who don't celebrate Christmas Eve join us in the festivities. We have a vegan or two who really appreciate this salad and have plate after plate of it. It is a favorite every single time I make it.

gluten free

vegan

What you'll need

2 small heads Boston or Bibb lettuce

1 medium red onion, thinly sliced

1 large tomato, quartered

6 to 8 radishes, thinly sliced

¼ cup red wine vinegar

1 teaspoon salt or more to taste

½ teaspoon pepper

½ teaspoon sugar

½ teaspoon sweet or smoked paprika

½ teaspoon dried oregano leaves

½ cup olive oil

What you'll do

Tear the lettuce into small pieces and place it in a salad bowl. Layer the onion, tomato, and radishes on top of the lettuce.

Whisk together the vinegar, salt, pepper, sugar, paprika, and oregano in a small bowl. Continue whisking as you add the olive oil in a slow, steady stream. Whisk until all ingredients are combined. Pour the dressing over the salad and serve.

This salad is just the right prelude to many Cuban dishes. The creaminess of ripe avocados and the tanginess of the vinegar-based dressing complement many of our hearty savory dishes perfectly.

gluten free

vegan

What you'll need

¼ cup red wine vinegar

½ teaspoon salt

¼ teaspoon white pepper

¼ cup olive oil

1 large or 2 small ripe avocados, peeled and cut into 1- to 2-inch chunks

1 medium red onion, very thinly sliced

What you'll do

Whisk together the vinegar, salt, and white pepper in a small bowl. Continue whisking as you add the olive oil in a slow, steady stream.

Arrange the avocado on a platter, then top with slices of onion. Pour the dressing over the salad and serve immediately.

Cuban Potato Salad

I love potato salad. However, I detest the store-bought, deli-style, preservative-ridden potato salad that most people consume. Potato salad is easy to make and the effort is evident in the final product. This is great with Cuban-Style Fried Chicken (page 103) or all on its own. I remember making it with Michael Symon and Daphne Oz on ABC's show *The Chew* and everyone just loved it.

gluten free

vegetarian

What you'll need

2 pounds red potatoes, peeled and cut into 2-inch cubes

4 ounces cream cheese, softened

½ cup mayonnaise (I like Hellmann's)

½ cup Miracle Whip

½ cup minced onion

½ cup diced pimentos

½ cup canned peas, drained

1 teaspoon Dijon mustard

1 tablespoon red wine vinegar

Salt and white pepper

What you'll do

At least 2 hours in advance, place the potatoes with water to cover in a pan over medium-high heat. Bring the water to a boil and let the potatoes boil for 15 to 20 minutes, until they are fork-tender. Drain the potatoes, transfer them to a bowl, and refrigerate them for at least 1 hour.

After the potatoes have chilled, combine the cream cheese, mayonnaise, and Miracle Whip in a large bowl. Using an electric mixer on low speed or a fork, mix until the ingredients are fully combined and no lumps are visible. Add the onion, pimentos, peas, mustard, vinegar, and salt and pepper to taste. Mix well.

Add the chilled potatoes and toss well, preferably with clean hands to avoid breaking up the potatoes. Taste the salad and adjust the seasonings, if necessary. Serve chilled.

Store in an airtight container in the refrigerator for up to 3 days.

Chicken Salad

Before you get excited about the diet potential of this salad, let me clear up a few things. First, this is not a "light" salad of greens with a grilled chicken breast on top. It is a concoction of sorts; a delicious combination of ingredients held together by copious amounts of mayonnaise. But here's a tip: If your chicken is well seasoned you can totally get away with half the mayo the recipe calls for. Nevertheless, if you have ever had truly homemade *ensalada de pollo,* you will not perceive it as something that could wreak havoc on your waistline, but as comfort food at its best. I do not remember a single party from my youth that did not involve somebody's version of this salad. Of course, my mom's version is the absolute best. It requires a little time and a lot of chopping, but it is worth every ounce of effort. And mayonnaise.

You may wish to decorate the bowl in which you serve the salad by lining it with romaine lettuce leaves and topping it with additional sliced hard-boiled egg, peas, and pimentos.

What you'll need

4 large red potatoes, peeled and cut into 1-inch cubes

1 cup mayonnaise, plus more as needed

1 tablespoon Dijon mustard

3 tablespoons diced pimentos

1 tablespoon red wine vinegar

1 tablespoon sugar

Salt and pepper

1 whole roasted chicken, skinned, pulled off the bone, and finely chopped

1 large green apple, peeled, cored, and cut into ½-inch cubes

3 large hard-boiled eggs, chopped

¾ cup canned peas (reserve ¼ cup of the liquid)

What you'll do

Place the potatoes in a pot with just enough salted water to cover and bring to a boil. Continue boiling, uncovered, for 15 to 20 minutes, until the potatoes are fork-tender. Drain and set aside.

In a large bowl, whisk together the mayonnaise, mustard, reserved pea liquid, vinegar, sugar, and salt and pepper to taste. Add the chicken and stir well. Taste the salad and adjust the seasonings, if necessary.

Add the apple, eggs, peas, and pimentos, and toss the salad with your hands to prevent the eggs and soft vegetables from breaking apart. If the salad looks too dry, add a couple more tablespoons of mayonnaise.

Store in an airtight container in the refrigerator for up to 3 days.

CINCO

ALL THINGS RICE

There is no denying that Cubans are genetically predisposed to consuming large quantities of carbohydrates. While we do love our starchy root vegetables and our Cuban bread, no meal is really complete without rice. Rice is the mainstay, the foundation, the life force if you will, of Cuban cuisine. Rice is a nonnegotiable part of our everyday meals. Sure, we've tried to reduce our intake of this big bad carb. We have even attempted in vain to eliminate it altogether. But what would a big bowl of black beans be without this tasty grain we call rice? And bonus—it's gluten free!

Rice dishes can be stored in the refrigerator for up to 3 days.

White Rice

gluten free

vegan

Because the only thing you need to make rice in an automatic rice cooker is the instruction booklet, I will only provide you with the recipe for rice made the traditional way. And don't worry, its actually easier than you think.

What you'll need

1½ teaspoons salt

1 cup long-grain white rice (I like Mahatma brand)

2 tablespoons vegetable, corn, or canola oil

What you'll do

Bring 2 cups cold water to a boil in a medium-sized saucepan. Add the salt, rice, and oil. Continue boiling for 2 minutes. Reduce heat to low, stir in the rice, cover the pan, and let the rice simmer for 20 to 25 minutes, until almost all of the liquid has been soaked up by the rice. Remove the pan from the heat, fluff the rice with a fork, and add additional salt, if necessary.

Arroz con Mariscos

Seafood Rice

Serves 6 to 8

pescatarian

gluten free

What you'll need

1 pound large shrimp, peeled and deveined (reserve shells)

2 medium lobster tails removed from the shell, deveined and cut into 2-inch discs (reserve shells)

5 cups Shrimp and Lobster Stock (see recipe below)

½ cup olive oil

1 pound firm white fish fillets, such as grouper or snapper, cut into 3- to 4-inch pieces

1 pound fresh littleneck clams or mussels or ½ pound of each

4 garlic cloves, minced

1 medium green bell pepper, chopped

1 large onion, chopped

1 cup canned tomato sauce

1 bay leaf

½ cup *vino seco* (dry white cooking wine)

1 tablespoon red wine vinegar

½ teaspoon ground oregano

½ teaspoon ground cumin

1½ teaspoons *Bijol* (yellow food coloring and seasoning; see Glossary, page 170)

1½ teaspoons salt, plus more as needed

½ teaspoon pepper, plus more as needed

2 cups Valencia or short-grain rice

½ cup canned peas, for garnish

½ cup diced pimentos, for garnish

What you'll do

Peel and devein the shrimp, reserving the shells for the stock. Remove the lobster tails from their shells; reserve the shells for the stock.

Heat the olive oil in a large pot or Dutch oven over medium-high heat. Add the shrimp and sauté until opaque, 3 to 4 minutes. Set aside.

Heat the olive oil in a large pot or Dutch oven over medium-high heat sauté the garlic, bell pepper, and onion for 5 to 7 minutes, until the onion is translucent. Add the tomato sauce, bay leaf, *vino seco,* vinegar, oregano, cumin, *Bijol,* salt, pepper, and stock, and bring to a boil. Add the rice and cook, uncovered, for 5 minutes. Reduce the heat to low and add the shrimp, lobster, clams or mussels and the fish carefully to the pot. The seafood should be submerged in at least 2 to 3 inches of stock (add additional stock if necessary). Cover the pot, and cook for 17 to 20 minutes, until the rice becomes tender. Taste and adjust the seasoning, if necessary. Remove and discard the bay leaf. Garnish with peas and pimentos.

Tip: Box stock is fine for this recipe but in that case I prefer vegetable or chicken stock. You may use box stock and add just the shrimp shells and boil for 20 or 30 minutes to give it that seafood essence.

Shrimp and Lobster Stock

What you'll need

2 bay leaves

1 tablespoon salt

½ teaspoon freshly ground pepper

½ lemon, cut in half

1 medium onion, peeled and quartered

Shrimp shells (see ingredient list for the rice)

Lobster shells (see ingredient list for the rice)

What you'll do

To make the stock, bring 10 cups of water to a boil in a large stockpot over medium-high heat.

Carefully add the bay leaves, pepper, lemon, onion, and reserved shrimp and lobster shells. Continue to boil for 20 to 30 minutes, uncovered. Reduce heat to low, cover, and simmer for an additional 3 hours.

Allow the stock to cool a bit before straining. Reserve the 5 cups you will need for this recipe and refrigerate or freeze the remaining stock for future use.

Cuban-Style Fried Rice

Many people don't know that Cuba always had a pretty substantial number of Chinese immigrants. In fact, there is even a Chinatown called *El Barrio Chino*. I couldn't ignore the Chinese influence on Cuban cuisine in this book, particularly since my grandfather was one of the thousands of Chinese who immigrated to Cuba in the early 1900s. This was his recipe for fried rice. I've omitted the MSG he insisted on adding to all his dishes. You can thank me later!

What you'll need

12 medium shrimp

2 tablespoons canola or peanut oil

2 garlic cloves, minced

½ cup diced onion

¼ cup diced scallions

2 cups cold *Arroz Blanco* (White Rice; page 70), preferably cooked the day before

¼ cup sweet deli-style ham, chopped

2 large eggs, scrambled

2 tablespoons low-sodium soy sauce, plus more as needed

6 slices bacon, fried crisp and crumbled

What you'll do

Pour 3 cups of lightly salted water into a large pan and bring to a boil. Add the shrimp and boil for 2 to 3 minutes, until the shrimp are opaque. Drain the shrimp and set them aside to cool. Peel, devein, and cut the tails off the shrimp. Set aside.

Heat the oil in a large frying pan or wok over medium-high heat. Working quickly, add the garlic, onion, and scallions. Stir continuously for 3 minutes, then add the rice, ham, and eggs. Cook, stirring, making sure the mixture is heated through and the rice is actually frying. Add half the soy sauce and stir so it is equally distributed. Add the bacon, shrimp, and the rest of the soy sauce, and continue frying, adjusting the heat as necessary. Taste the rice and add additional soy sauce, if needed. Serve immediately.

Note: For a vegetarian alternative, omit the protein.

For a gluten-free alternative, substitute gluten-free tamari for the soy sauce, available at most grocery stores.

For a vegan alternative: Omit protein and eggs, and substitute gluten-free tamari for the soy sauce.

Red Beans and Rice

Serves 6 to 8

gluten free

Growing up, I was always terribly confused by the Spanish dishes *Congri* and *Moros* (page 76). My mom, who will not admit it, often used the titles interchangeably, thereby contributing to my confusion. Just to clarify, *Congri* are red beans with rice, while *Moros* are black beans with rice and both are absolutely divine.

What you'll need

½ pound dried red beans, rinsed, and soaked overnight

1 bay leaf

½ pound bacon, chopped

4 tablespoons olive oil

1 green bell pepper, chopped

2 medium onions, chopped

3 garlic cloves, minced

1 pound long-grain white rice

1 teaspoon ground oregano

½ teaspoon ground cumin

½ teaspoon white pepper

Salt

What you'll do

Place a medium to large sieve over a large bowl and drain the beans into the sieve, catching the soaking water in the bowl underneath. Use a measuring cup to measure the soaking water as you transfer it to a large pot. Add additional water, if necessary, to equal 5 cups. Add the beans and bay leaf and bring the water to a boil over high heat.

Reduce the heat to low, cover the pot, and let the beans simmer for about 2 hours, until they are fork-tender. Let the beans cool to room temperature, then drain them, reserving 3 cups of their cooking liquid. Remove and discard the bay leaf. Set aside.

Cook the bacon in the same pot over medium heat until it is crisp, 5 to 7 minutes. Discard half the rendered fat, then add half the olive oil, the bell pepper, onions, and garlic. Sauté for 5 to 7 minutes, until the vegetables are soft and caramelized. Add the rice, the 3 cups reserved liquid, and the oregano, cumin, pepper, and salt to taste, and bring to a boil; boil for 5 minutes.

Meanwhile, combine the beans with the remaining olive oil in a bowl and season with salt to taste. Add to the rice mixture, then boil, uncovered, for 10 minutes, until most of the water is absorbed by the rice. Reduce the heat to low, cover the pot, and let the beans and rice simmer for an additional 15 to 20 minutes, until all the liquid is absorbed. Fluff the rice with a fork, taste, and adjust the seasonings, if necessary.

Note: For a vegetarian alternative, omit the animal protein.

vegeta
ALTERN

Black Beans and Rice

Serves 6 to 8

gluten free

This recipe is made exactly like *Congri,* except instead of bacon, the recipe calls for pork shoulder or leg. If you want to use pork tenderloin, cook a quarter pound of bacon and use the rendered fat (not the actual bacon) to cook the tenderloin chunks.

What you'll need

½ pound dried black beans, rinsed and soaked overnight

1 teaspoon salt, plus more as needed

1 bay leaf

¼ cup plus 2 tablespoons olive oil

¼ pound cooked bacon (you may substitute turkey bacon)

1 green bell pepper, chopped

2 medium onions, chopped

3 garlic cloves, minced

1 pound long-grain white rice

1 teaspoon ground oregano

½ teaspoon ground cumin

½ teaspoon white pepper

What you'll do

Place a medium or large sieve over a large bowl and drain the beans into the sieve, catching the soaking water in the bowl underneath.

Use a measuring cup to measure the soaking water as you transfer it to a large pot. Add additional water, if necessary, to equal 5 cups. Add the beans, salt, and bay leaf and bring the water to a boil over high heat. Reduce the heat to low, cover the pot, and let the beans simmer for about 2 hours, or until they are fork-tender.

Let the beans cool to room temperature, then drain them, reserving 3 cups of their cooking liquid. Remove and discard the bay leaf. Set aside.

Heat 2 tablespoons of the olive oil in the same pot over medium-high heat. Add the bacon and cook over medium heat 5 to 7 minutes, until the bacon browns, is lightly crispy, and renders most of its fat.

Discard half the fat, then add another 2 tablespoons of the olive oil, the bell pepper, onions, and garlic, and sauté for 5 to 7 minutes, until the vegetables are soft and caramelized. Add the rice, the 3 cups reserved liquid, the oregano, cumin, and pepper and bring to a boil; boil for 5 minutes.

Meanwhile, combine the beans with the remaining 2 tablespoons olive oil and season with salt to taste. Add to the rice mixture and continue boiling, uncovered, for 10 minutes, until most of the water is absorbed by the rice.

Reduce the heat to low, cover the pot, and let the beans and rice simmer for an additional 15 to 20 minutes, until all the liquid is absorbed. Fluff the rice with a fork, taste, and adjust the seasonings, if necessary.

Note: For a vegetarian alternative, omit the animal protein.

vegetar
ALTERNA

Yellow Rice

I just adore yellow rice. It is a great base for so many dishes. I love it on its own, as well as with black beans, which isn't very Cuban of me. Many of you might not know that Cubans consider it very American to eat yellow rice with black beans. It's just never done. But I say don't knock it until you've tried it. Trust me, it's good.

gluten free

What you'll need

¼ cup olive oil

1 medium onion, diced

2 garlic cloves, minced

2 cups long-grain white rice (I like Uncle Ben's converted rice for this recipe)

1½ teaspoons *Bijol* (yellow food coloring and seasoning; see Glossary, page 170)

4 cups low-sodium chicken stock

Salt and pepper

What you'll do

Heat the olive oil in a large saucepan over medium heat. Add the onion and garlic, and sauté for 5 to 7 minutes, until the onion is translucent. Be careful not to brown the onion.

Add the rice and stir well. Add the *Bijol* and stock and stir to incorporate. Bring the mixture to a boil and cook, uncovered, for 5 minutes. Reduce the heat to low, fluff the rice with a fork, cover the pan, and continue cooking for 17 to 20 minutes, until the rice is tender and fluffy. Taste the rice and add salt and pepper to taste.

Note: For a vegetarian/vegan alternative, substitute vegetable stock for the chicken stock.

vegan/ vegetarian ALTERNATIVE

Chooken and Rice

After black beans, this is perhaps the most requested dish at any Cuban restaurant. You should know that nothing—and I mean *nothing*—compares to homemade *arroz con pollo.* The dry, pale, yellow rice with the equally dismal-looking chicken that is served at most restaurants and "food by the pound" places are not what we will be making here. The homemade result is substantially more satisfying.

What you'll need

¼ cup olive oil

1 whole chicken, cut into 8 pieces, or 4 or 5 large, bone-in skinless chicken breasts

Salt and pepper

3 garlic cloves, minced

1 large onion, chopped

1 medium green bell pepper, chopped

1 (8-ounce) can tomato sauce

2 (5-gram) packets annatto seasoning mix (I prefer Goya *Sazón con Azafrán*)

1 bay leaf

1 cup *vino seco* (dry white cooking wine), or 1 (12-ounce) can beer

2 cups Valencia or other short-grain rice

6 cups chicken stock

1 (8.5-ounce) can peas (do not drain)

1 (8.5-ounce) can roasted red peppers

Tostones (Fried Green Plantains; page 125) or *Mariquitas* (Plantain Chips; page 16), for serving

What you'll do

Heat the olive oil in a large Dutch oven or ovenproof pot over medium to medium-high heat.

Season the chicken generously with salt and pepper, then add it to the pot in batches and sear it, skin side down, for 3 to 5 minutes, until lightly browned. Do not turn it too soon, as it will stick. Be careful not to crowd the pan. (Putting too many pieces of chicken in the pot at once will cause the heat to dissipate, and you'll end up with steamed chicken.) Transfer the chicken to a plate and set aside.

Add the garlic, onion, and bell pepper to the same pot and sauté for about 10 minutes, until soft. Add the tomato sauce and let it simmer for 5 minutes. Add the annatto seasoning, bay leaf, and *vino seco,* and cook for 5 minutes more.

Add the rice and stir until it is fully incorporated into the tomato mixture. Add 4 cups of the stock and the liquid from the canned peas and stir. Add the chicken and top with as much of the remaining 2 cups stock as your pot will allow while leaving about 3 inches of space at the top of the pot. Bring to a boil, cover, and reduce the heat to low. Cook for 10 to 15 minutes.

Preheat the oven to 325°F.

Transfer the entire pot, lid and all, to the oven. (If your pot has a plastic handle, wrap it in foil to protect it from the oven's heat.) Bake for at least 40 minutes, until the grains expand and the rice is uniformly cooked. The liquid need not be fully absorbed for the rice to be ready. You can cook this longer, depending on how soupy (*a la chorrera*) you like it. Remember that the liquid continues to evaporate with the residual heat, even once out of the oven, so take out the chicken and rice when it is a little soupier than you want it to be. Remove and discard the bay leaf.

Decorate the top of the rice with the peas and red peppers and serve with the *tostones* or *mariquitas*.

Chicken and Rice Casserole

Serves 6 to 8

Almost everyone has tried *arroz con pollo* (chicken and rice). *Arroz imperial* is basically *arroz con pollo* in casserole form. Like a lasagna it is prepared in layers: Rice alternating with chicken, then finished off with a layer of cheese and a thin coat of mayonnaise (trust me, it's good). The result is a great make-ahead party dish that only requires a fork and a hearty appetite to enjoy.

What you'll need

¼ cup olive oil

1 large onion, diced

1 medium green bell pepper, diced

3 garlic cloves, minced

1½ cups canned tomato sauce

¼ cup *vino seco* (dry white cooking wine)

1 bay leaf

1 whole chicken, roasted, bones and skin removed, meat chopped

3½ cups low-sodium chicken stock

1½ teaspoons *Bijol* (yellow food coloring and seasoning; see Glossary, page 170)

2 cups long-grain white rice

½ cup freshly grated Parmesan cheese

1 cup mayonnaise (I prefer Hellman's)

Salt and pepper

Tostones (Fried Green Plantains; page 125), for serving

What you'll do

Heat the olive oil in a large saucepan over medium heat. Add the onion, bell pepper, and garlic, and sauté for 5 to 7 minutes, until the onions are translucent. Be careful not to brown the vegetables. Add the tomato sauce,

vino seco, and bay leaf, and cook for another 5 minutes. Add the chicken, stir well, and cook for 3 minutes. Remove from the heat and set aside. Remove and discard the bay leaf.

Bring the stock to a boil over high heat in a large saucepan. Add the *Bijol* and rice, then bring the mixture to a boil again. Cook, uncovered, for 5 minutes. Reduce the heat to low, fluff the rice with a fork, cover the pan, and cook for 17 to 20 minutes, until the rice is tender and fluffy. Taste the rice and season with salt and pepper to taste.

Preheat the oven to 375°F.

Butter the bottom and sides of a 3-quart rectangular casserole dish. Spread a thin layer of rice, about ¼-inch thick, in the dish, then add a layer of the chicken mixture. Spread half the remaining rice on top of the chicken, then spread the remaining chicken mixture on top of that. Top the layers with the remaining rice.

Combine the Parmesan cheese with the mayonnaise and spread it evenly across the top of the casserole.

Bake the casserole for 10 to 15 minutes, until the top of the casserole is lightly browned. Serve with the *tostones.*

Arroz con Huevos Fritos

White Rice and Fried Eggs

Serves 1

This meal is a childhood favorite. It's the dish most Cuban moms make when their cupboards are bare. It became very popular when Cuban families first immigrated to America, because it is so inexpensive to make and kids just love it! No matter what you have in your cupboards, a steaming bowl of rice topped with fried eggs hits the spot every time.

gluten free

vegetarian

What you'll need

¼ cup corn or canola oil

1 cup *Arroz Blanco* (White Rice; page 70)

2 large eggs

Salt and pepper

What you'll do

Heat the oil in a large frying pan over medium-high heat.

Place the rice in a bowl or mound it on a small plate.

Working with one egg at a time, crack the eggs into a small bowl, pour them into the hot oil, and fry them until they are somewhat firm but still soft in the middle. Carefully spoon some hot oil on top of the egg to cook it slightly, creating a thin white film.

Using a large, slotted spoon, remove the eggs from the oil and drain them over a paper towel before placing them on top of the rice. Season with salt and pepper to taste.

SEIS

MAIN COURSES

Meat, Fish, and Everything in Between

There are few things Cubans enjoy more than pork. Wait, let me rephrase that. There is *nothing* Cubans enjoy more than pork. Fried pork chunks, smoked pork chops, pork ribs, pork sandwiches, pork rinds, and—of course, the crowning glory, the king of all meat and the rite of passage to Cuban manhood—*el lechón asado*: the whole roasted pig. Perhaps Cubans embraced this protein since pigs are easier and more economical to raise than cattle and require less land to roam. I mean, we are practical people after all. And fun fact, according to some sources, hogs were brought to Cuba by Christopher Columbus.

There is no denying that Cuban food is protein focused. Probably because someone's uncle who was a doctor in Cuba insisted that not having a steak regularly would cause anemia, or scurvy, or a slew of other ailments. Today we know that lean meats are good for you, and that there are many meat alternatives that are healthy and tasty too.

Picadillo

Savory Beef Hash   Serves 4 to 6

gluten free

Picadillo is super versatile. Sometimes I make it the traditional way, sometimes I make it with ground turkey breast with dried cranberries and almonds, and sometimes . . . wait for it, I make a vegan version that uses ground walnuts in place of the meat, cooked in a savory *sofrito* with all the traditional fixings that won't leave you wondering "where's the beef"!?

What you'll need

4 tablespoons olive oil

1 medium onion, diced

1 small green bell pepper, diced

1 pound ground sirloin or ground round (you may substitute ground turkey for the beef)

½ cup *vino seco* (dry white cooking wine)

1 cup canned tomato sauce

2 tablespoons tomato paste

½ teaspoon ground cumin

½ teaspoon ground oregano

1 teaspoon salt

½ teaspoon black pepper

¼ cup raisins, optional

¼ cup roughly chopped pimento-stuffed olives

2 tablespoons capers

What you'll do

To make the *picadillo*, heat 2 tablespoons of the olive oil in a large frying pan over medium-high heat. Add the garlic, onion, and bell pepper and sauté until tender, 5 to 7 minutes. Raise the heat to medium-high and add the ground beef. (The meat should make a searing sound when it hits the pan—use a small amount of meat to test the heat level; if it doesn't sizzle, increase the heat to high for a few minutes before adding the meat.) Stir to break up any large chunks of meat, and cook

for 3 to 5 minutes, stirring frequently, until the beef is thoroughly cooked (no longer red). Drain any excess liquid from the pan.

Add the *vino seco,* tomato sauce, tomato paste, cumin, oregano, salt, pepper, and the remaining 2 tablespoons olive oil. Reduce the heat to low and simmer, uncovered, for about 20 minutes.

Add the raisins, olives, and capers and stir to combine. Serve with white rice, brown rice, polenta, or quinoa or in tacos.

Store leftovers, covered, in the refrigerator for up to 3 days.

Note: For keto, vegan, and vegetarian alternatives, roughly crushed walnuts make an excellent meat substitute for picadillo. Just substitute 16 ounces of crushed walnuts for the meat in the recipe. You can also substitute a pound of Impossible ground meat for the ground beef. Omit the raisins for a keto-friendly version.

vegan vegetar *ALTERNA*

keto friend *ALTERNA*

Variation: *Picadillo de Pavo con Almendras y Arandanos Secos*

Turkey Picadillo with Almonds and Dried Cranberries

Follow recipe for picadillo above, substituting ground turkey for the ground beef. Add ¼ cup sliced or slivered almonds and ¼ cup dried cranberries; omit the olives, capers, and raisins.

Roast Pork Leg

I love this recipe because it is so low maintenance. I mean, you virtually ignore it once you get it in the oven. Plan ahead though, because you will need to start preparing two full days before you intend to serve this Cuban staple. This pork marinates for 24 hours, and then cooks slowly in your oven for another 24 hours on top of that. So be forewarned.

This recipe calls for a leg of pork, but pork shoulder works nicely too.

What you'll need

2 cups sour orange juice (from 8 to 10 oranges) or a mixture of equal parts lime juice and orange juice

15 garlic cloves, minced

2 medium onions, thinly sliced

½ cup olive oil

1 tablespoon dried oregano leaves

1 tablespoon ground cumin

2 teaspoons white pepper

4 tablespoons coarse salt

1 (8- to 10-pound) pork leg or shoulder

What you'll do

Combine the orange juice, garlic, onions, olive oil, oregano, cumin, pepper, and 1 tablespoon of the salt in a large bowl and give it a stir.

Rinse and dry the pork, then rub it all over with the remaining 3 tablespoons of salt. Place the pork in a high-sided roasting pan that will fit in your refrigerator. Pour half the orange juice mixture over the pork, cover it with foil, and refrigerate it overnight, turning the pork over after about 8 hours so both sides have an opportunity to soak up the marinade. Refrigerate the remaining orange juice mixture in an airtight container.

The following day, remove the pork from refrigerator and preheat the oven to 400°F. Bake the pork, uncovered, for 30 minutes. Then reduce the heat to 175°F, cover the roasting pan with foil, and let the pig roast for at least 17 hours, or up to 22 hours.

Two hours before serving, remove the foil and increase the oven temperature to 375°F. Continue roasting the pork for 2 more hours. Remove the pork from the oven and let it to rest in the pan for 30 minutes. While the pork rests, bring the reserved orange juice mixture to a boil in a small saucepan. Boil for 3 to 5 minutes, until the garlic softens. To serve, carve the roast—although most of the time, carving won't be necessary, as the meat will just fall off the bone—and pour the warmed marinade over the pork.

Bistec de Palomilla

Minute Steak

This is the quintessential Cuban beef dish. It is usually served with white rice and *plátanitos maduros* (fried sweet plantains) or French fries and garnished with raw onions and parsley at every Cuban restaurant, cafeteria, and hole-in-the-wall eatery. Typically, the cuts of beef used are a quarter-inch-thin top round or sirloin steaks, although you could start with a thicker cut of beef and just pound it thin with a meat mallet before cooking.

gluten free

keto friendly

What you'll need

¼ cup sour orange juice or a mixture of equal parts lime juice and orange juice

1 garlic clove, crushed

4 (¼-inch-thick) sirloin or top round steaks

Garlic powder (not garlic salt)

¼ teaspoon salt, plus more as needed

Black pepper

2 tablespoons olive oil

1 cup chopped onion

¼ cup chopped fresh parsley

1 tablespoon fresh lime juice

Arroz Blanco (White Rice; page 70), for serving

Plátanitos Maduros (Fried Sweet Plantains; page 122), for serving

What you'll do

Combine the orange juice and garlic in a small bowl.

Arrange the steaks in a shallow, nonreactive dish and pour the orange juice mixture over them. Marinate the steaks at room temperature for 15 to 30 minutes—no longer or they will turn an unappealing grayish hue. Also, because the steaks are so thin, they won't need any longer for the tanginess of the sour orange to penetrate them.

Discard the marinade, pat the steaks dry with paper towels, and season the steaks with garlic powder, salt, and pepper.

Heat 1 tablespoon of the olive oil in a cast iron pan until the oil is almost smoking. Carefully fry the steaks, one at a time, for about 2 minutes on each side. Transfer the cooked steak to a plate and continue with the remaining steaks, letting the pan return to a high temperature after each steak. Add the remaining tablespoon of olive oil to the pan before frying the third and fourth steaks.

Combine the onion, parsley, lime juice, and ¼ teaspoon salt in a small bowl and give it a quick stir. Garnish each steak with the onion–parsley mixture and serve with the white rice and *tostones*.

Shredded Beef in Tomato Sauce

Serves 6 to 8

I just adore *ropa vieja*—I order it almost every time I eat at a Cuban restaurant. I love it with white rice *and* black beans all mixed together on one plate. The name, which means *old clothes*, really doesn't do the dish justice and may intimidate some people from trying it. Therefore, I recommend that you not translate its name for any of your non-Spanish-speaking friends. Just tell them it is one of those Spanish terms that do not translate well. If they don't buy that, at least wait until after they take a bite to divulge the name of this classic Cuban dish. For this dish, you'll boil flank steak until it is extremely tender, then shred it and sauté in a savory *sofrito* with peas and pimentos. The combination is just divine.

What you'll need

2 teaspoons salt, plus more as needed

1 tablespoon whole black peppercorns

2 pounds flank steak

½ cup olive oil

3 garlic cloves, minced

1 medium onion, roughly chopped

1 medium green bell pepper, roughly chopped

1 medium red bell pepper, roughly chopped

2 cups canned tomato sauce

1 bay leaf

½ teaspoon white pepper

1 cup *vino seco* (dry white cooking wine)

½ cup canned peas, for garnish

¼ cup chopped pimentos, for garnish

What you'll do

Combine 1½ quarts of water, 1 teaspoon of the salt, and the peppercorns in a large pot and bring to a boil over high heat. Add the steak and reduce the heat to low. Cover the pot and cook for about 2 hours, until the meat is nice and tender.

Heat the olive oil in a large frying pan over medium heat. Add the garlic, onion, and bell peppers and sauté for about 10 minutes, until the vegetables are soft. Add the tomato sauce, bay leaf, white pepper, and remaining teaspoon of salt, and bring the mixture to a boil. Add the *vino seco* and continue boiling for 5 minutes. Reduce the heat to low and simmer for 20 minutes. Remove the pan from the heat and set aside.

Drain the flank steak and let it cool to room temperature on a plate lined with paper towels. Use your hands to shred the beef into long strips; if you shred it along the grain, it should come apart easily. Season the steak with salt and pepper and add it to the tomato mixture. Stir to coat the meat with the sauce. Cook over medium-low heat for a minimum of 20 to 30 minutes, to allow the flavors to come together. Remove and discard the bay leaf.

Garnish with peas and pimentos before serving.

Store leftovers, covered, in the refrigerator for up to 3 days.

Vegan Variation: *Jackfruit Ropa Vieja*

What you'll need

1 medium onion

½ red bell pepper

1 jalapeño pepper

5–6 cloves garlic

1 tablespoon olive oil

¼ cup canned tomato sauce

½ teaspoon salt

1 teaspoon ground cumin

½ bay leaf

1 (20-ounce) can green jackfruit

½ cup vegetable broth

1 teaspoon soy sauce (for gluten-free variation, use tamari or gluten-free soy sauce)

Small handful fresh cilantro, chopped, for garnish

vegan

gluten free

What you'll do

Cut the onion lengthwise in half and remove the peel. Cut each half lengthwise into slices so you get lots of onion strips. Remove the seeds and membranes from the bell pepper and cut into strips. Cut the jalapeño into strips (I leave the seeds/membranes for heat). Mince enough garlic to get 1 tablespoon.

Heat the olive oil in a large, heavy skillet (cast iron if you have it) over medium-high heat. Add the onion and tomato sauce and cook for about 10 minutes, stirring occasionally. After 5 minutes, the onions should be softened. Allow the tomato sauce to thicken and caramelize for another 5 minutes. During the final few minutes, you will need to stir frequently to prevent the sauce from burning. Stir in the salt, cumin, and the half bay leaf and cook for another minute, until the onions are browned. Stir in the peppers and garlic and reduce the heat to low.

Drain the jackfruit and shred or chop it finely. Add the jackfruit and vegetable broth to the skillet and stir. Cover and simmer for 20 minutes.

Remove the lid and simmer until the sauce thickens. Discard the bay leaf. Stir in the soy sauce and taste for salt.

This tastes best if made several hours or a day before serving to allow flavors to marry. Top with cilantro at serving time.

Beef Stew

Serves 6 to 8

When a Cuban hears "meat and potatoes," she thinks *carne con papas*. After all, that *is* the exact translation. So, while the idea of meat and potatoes would conjure up an image of a T-bone steak and a baked potato for many Americans, a Cuban or Cuban American will pine away for this savory and delectable stew. Like many Cuban recipes, this dish makes great leftovers and can even be made a day or two ahead. In fact, it tastes even better the next day.

What you'll need

½ cup olive oil

2 pounds top round, eye of the round, or boneless chuck roast, cut into 1- to 2-inch chunks

1 teaspoon salt

½ teaspoon black pepper

3 garlic cloves, minced

1 medium green bell pepper, chopped

1 onion, chopped

2 cups canned tomato sauce

2 cups beef stock

1 bay leaf

1 cup *vino seco* (dry white cooking wine)

4 carrots, peeled and cut into 1-inch pieces

1 pound red or white potatoes, peeled and cut into 2-inch cubes

½ cup pimento-stuffed olives

What you'll do

Heat the olive oil in a large pot over medium-high heat. Pat the beef dry with a paper towel and season generously with the salt and pepper. Add the beef, in small batches, to the hot oil and brown it on all sides. Transfer the browned meat to a plate and set aside.

Reduce the heat to medium, add the garlic, bell pepper, and onion to the pot, and sauté for 5 to 7 minutes, until soft. Add the tomato sauce, stock, bay leaf, and *vino seco,* raise the heat to high, and bring to a boil. Let the stew boil, uncovered, for 10 minutes, until the sauce reduces by a quarter.

Add the carrots, potatoes, and beef, reduce the heat to low, and cover the pot. Let the stew simmer for about 1½ hours, stirring occasionally, until the vegetables are soft and the meat is tender. Add the olives and taste; adjust the seasonings, if necessary. Remove and discard the bay leaf.

I recommend you drizzle a little olive oil into each bowl of this delectable dish just before you serve it.

Store leftovers, covered, in the refrigerator for up to 3 days.

Note: For a keto-friendly alternative, substitute parsnips for the potatoes. Incorporate into the recipe in the same manner as the potatoes. Parsnips will need an additional 10 minutes to become tender so allow for extra cooking time.

keto
friend

ALTERNA

Meatloaf

Serves 6 to 8

Wait a minute! Do not turn the page or stop reading! This is no ordinary meatloaf. It is not even close to the gray-hued, crumbly, dry brick that perhaps you've sadly grown accustomed to. This is moist and flavorful. It's not even oven-baked in a loaf pan. It is shaped by hand and slowly simmered in a delicious tangy tomato sauce infused with garlic, bell pepper, and onion. The meat is delicately formed around hard-boiled eggs so that when sliced, a tasty surprise is revealed.

What you'll need

1 pound ground sirloin

½ pound ground pork

½ pound ground sweet ham, such as honey or maple glazed ham (see Note below)

2 teaspoons salt

1 teaspoon black pepper

½ teaspoon dried oregano leaves

1 teaspoon sweet or smoked paprika

1 large egg, beaten

1 cup dry seasoned breadcrumbs

4 large hard-boiled eggs

½ cup olive oil

4 garlic cloves, minced

1 medium green bell pepper, diced

1 large yellow onion, diced

2 cups canned tomato sauce

1 bay leaf

½ cup *vino seco* (dry white cooking wine)

½ cup canned peas (reserve liquid)

½ cup pimentos

What you'll do

Combine the beef, pork, and ham in a large bowl. Add 1 teaspoon of the salt, ½ teaspoon of the pepper, the oregano, and the paprika. Knead the meat lightly by hand until all of the ingredients are thoroughly combined. Add the egg and half the breadcrumbs and mix until thoroughly combined.

Transfer the meat mixture to a baking sheet and use your hands to shape it into one or two oblong or rectangular loaves. If this if your first time making this meatloaf, you might try making two smaller loaves instead of one larger one, as it's a little easier. Create a well in the center of the loaf. Carefully place the eggs in the well—all four if you are creating one loaf, or two in each of the two loaves—and fold the meat mixture over the eggs to enclose them entirely in the center of the loaf. Sprinkle the loaf with the remaining breadcrumbs to create a light coating, then pat the crumbs so they stick. Cover the loaf with plastic wrap, transfer the baking sheet to the refrigerator, and refrigerate for 1 hour.

Just before you take the meatloaf out of the refrigerator, heat the olive oil in a large pot over medium-high heat. Add the garlic, bell pepper, and onion, and sauté for about 10 minutes, until the vegetables are soft. Add the tomato sauce, bay leaf, *vino seco,* the remaining 1 teaspoon salt and ½ teaspoon pepper, and ¼ cup of the reserved pea liquid. Bring to a boil and cook for 5 minutes. Reduce the heat to low, cover the pot, and let the mixture simmer for 30 to 45 minutes.

While that cooks, remove the meatloaf from the refrigerator and let it warm up a bit.

Coat a large, shallow frying pan with nonstick cooking spray or olive or vegetable oil over medium-high heat. Carefully transfer the meatloaf to the pan and sear it on all sides, creating a golden crust. It is not necessary to cook the meat all the way through; just enough for it to firm up and remain stable.

Gently place the browned meatloaf in the pot with the tomato sauce mixture. Cover the pot, raise the heat to medium-low, and cook for 45 minutes to 1 hour. Spoon the sauce over the meat occasionally, but do not stir.

Carefully transfer the meat to a large platter and let it rest about 10 minutes before cutting it into slices.

To serve, pour tomato sauce over each serving and garnish with peas and pimentos.

Store leftovers, covered, in the refrigerator for up to 3 days.

Variation: *Albondigas*

Meatballs

Albondigas are a great variation on the meatloaf recipe, especially for parties. You can make them days in advance, and they are just as good hot as they are at room temperature. These meatballs also make amazing sandwiches. Warm Cuban bread, a few meatballs, a little sauce, and some thinly sliced onions, and you have one heck of a sandwich. Simply use the recipe above—omitting the hard-boiled eggs—and form meatballs of whatever size you want. Roll the meatballs lightly in the breadcrumbs, sear them on all sides, and add them to the tomato sauce, then cook as directed above.

Breaded Fried Steak

Serves 4

Bistec empanizado is like chicken-fried steak without the gravy. I've always been somewhat confused about chicken-fried steak—I mean, is it chicken or is it steak? It's steak, right?! So why not call it steak-fried steak? Or just breaded steak? Are you confused? I know I am. This breaded fried steak, named for what it is, is a Cuban classic. Serve it with *Moros* (Black Beans and Rice; page 76) and *Plátanitos Maduros* (Fried Sweet Plantains; page 122). Most people also enjoy it with a squeeze of lime.

What you'll need

¼ cup sour orange juice or a mixture of equal parts lime juice and orange juice

4 garlic cloves, minced

4 (¼-inch-thick) sirloin steaks

Salt and pepper

Olive oil, for shallow frying

4 large eggs, beaten

¾ cup finely ground cracker meal

¼ cup all-purpose flour

Lime wedges, for serving

What you'll do

Combine the orange juice and garlic in a small bowl.

Arrange the steaks in a shallow, nonreactive dish and pour the orange juice and garlic over them. Cover the steaks with plastic wrap and marinate them in the refrigerator for 1 hour. Drain the steaks, pat them dry, and season them liberally with salt and pepper.

Heat the olive oil in a large frying pan over medium-high heat. Place the eggs in a shallow bowl. Combine the cracker meal and flour in another shallow bowl. Dip the steaks in the egg, then in the flour mixture. Repeat this step, dipping the steak in the egg and flour mixture a second time. Shake off any excess flour and gently lay the steaks in the hot oil. Fry each steak individually for about 3 minutes on each side, until golden brown. Transfer the steaks to a paper towel–lined platter to drain.

Serve with a squeeze of lime.

Cuban Shepherd's Pie

Tambor is Spanish for "drum," and I suppose that if you made this dish in a round casserole, it could technically resemble a drum. Other than that, I'm not really sure why it is called *Tambor de Picadillo*. I like to think of this as Cuba's answer to shepherd's pie. Perhaps with a little more flavor.

What you'll need

For the Mashed Potatoes

3 pounds Yukon gold potatoes, peeled and cut into 2-inch pieces

6 garlic cloves

1 cup whole milk, warmed

4 tablespoons (½ stick) salted butter, melted

½ cup heavy cream, warmed

2 teaspoons salt, plus more if needed

½ teaspoon white pepper, plus more if needed

Picadillo

¼ cup olive oil

2 garlic cloves, minced

1 medium onion, diced

1 small green bell pepper, diced

1 pound ground sirloin or ground round

½ cup *vino seco* (dry white cooking wine)

1 cup canned tomato sauce

½ teaspoon ground cumin

½ teaspoon ground oregano

1 teaspoon salt

½ teaspoon black pepper

¼ cup raisins, optional

¼ cup pimento-stuffed olives, roughly chopped

2 tablespoons capers

½ cup grated Parmesan cheese

What you'll do

To make the mashed potatoes, bring 2 quarts of water to a boil in a large pot. Add the potatoes and whole garlic cloves. Reduce the heat to medium and cook the potatoes, partially covered, for 40 to 45 minutes, until they are fork-tender.

Combine the milk, butter, and cream in a bowl.

Drain the potatoes into a colander, remove and discard the garlic cloves, and return the potatoes to the pot. Using a handheld electric mixer, beat the potatoes until they break apart. Add the milk mixture little by little while still beating. Once all the ingredients are fully incorporated, add the salt and pepper. Taste and adjust the seasoning, if necessary. Set aside.

To make the *picadillo,* heat half the olive oil in a large frying pan over medium-high heat. Add the garlic, onion, and bell pepper and sauté for 5 to 7 minutes, until the vegetables are tender. Allow the pan to return to medium-high heat, then add a pinch of ground beef. The meat should make a searing sound when it hits the pan. Otherwise, increase the temperature to high for a few minutes. Add the beef when the pan is hot and sauté, breaking up large chunks of meat, for 10 to 15 minutes, until the beef is thoroughly cooked (no longer red). Drain any excess liquid from the pan.

Add the *vino seco,* tomato sauce, cumin, oregano, salt, pepper, and the remaining olive oil. Reduce the heat to low and simmer, uncovered, for 20 minutes, stirring occasionally, until the tomato sauce thickens slightly. Add the raisins, olives, and capers and set aside.

Preheat the oven to 350°F.

Layer half the mashed potatoes evenly on the bottom of a large, oiled or buttered ovenproof casserole dish. Cover the mashed potato layer with all the *picadillo.* Top with the remaining mashed potatoes. Finish the casserole by sprinkling the Parmesan cheese evenly over the top.

Bake for 20 to 25 minutes, until the top of the casserole turns a golden brown.

Store leftovers, covered, in the refrigerator for up to 3 days.

Note: For a vegetarian alternative, use Impossible meat or ground walnuts to make the picadillo.

vegetarian
ALTERNATIVE

Stir-Fried Beef (or Chicken)   Serves 6 to 8

Ok, technically this dish *is* what it says it is—beef, or *cow*, that is, in fact, *fried*. But like *Ropa Vieja* (Old Clothes; page 88), the translation of this recipe's name does not do the dish justice. When I was a little girl, I had visions of an entire cow (live, of course) being lowered into the world's largest pot of sizzling olive oil. . . . Yes, I participated in a twelve-step program to deal with these issues. I still love this dish, and I'm certain you will, too. Imagine perfectly seasoned and tender shredded flank fried until slightly crispy with onions and garlic.

Vaca Frita

Stir-Fried Beef

What you'll need

1 bay leaf

2 pounds flank steak

2 teaspoons salt

½ teaspoon black pepper

½ cup sour orange juice or a mixture of equal parts lime juice and orange juice

¼ cup olive oil

3 garlic cloves, minced

2 medium onions, thinly sliced

Lime wedges, optional

What you'll do

Bring 2 quarts of salted water to a boil in a large stockpot. Add the bay leaf and steak, then reduce the heat, cover the pot, and simmer for 2 hours.

Drain the flank steak and let it cool to room temperature on a plate lined with paper towels. Use your hands to shred the beef into long strips; if you shred it along the grain, it should come apart easily. Season the steak with salt and pepper, and place it in a shallow, nonreactive dish. Pour the orange and lime juices over the steak and let it marinate for at least 30 minutes. Drain the beef and set it aside.

Preheat a large cast iron skillet over medium-high heat. Add half the olive oil and heat it until it is almost smoking. Add half the garlic and half the steak and sauté, stirring frequently, for 7 to 10 minutes. Add half the onions and sauté for 5 minutes, until the edges of the beef become crispy. Transfer the mixture to a large plate and repeat this process with the remaining ingredients. Serve with white rice and lime wedges.

Variation: *Vaca Frita de Pollo*

Chicken Vaca Frita

Serves 6 to 8

Follow the recipe for beef vaca frita and substitute skinless bone-in chicken breast or skinless bone-in chicken thighs for the beef. Cook until very tender and allow to cool. Remove the chicken, debone, and shred into medium-sized pieces before proceeding with the recipe.

Tip: You may use boneless chicken for this, but I find that bone-in chicken stays more tender when boiled. As a bonus, you will have a great homemade stock that you can freeze and use later. Be sure to strain it and let it cool first. Freeze or use it within 3 days.

Cuban Pork Roast

Serves 4 to 6

This is another favorite from my childhood. It is our version of pot roast and it always hits the spot in the way only meat and potatoes can.

What you'll need

1 (3-pound) eye of round roast

½ pound ham steak cut into 1-inch pieces

½ teaspoon ground oregano

2 large bay leaves

1½ teaspoons salt or more to taste

½ teaspoon freshly ground black pepper

1½ cups Mojo Criollo (page 11)

¼ cup olive oil

2 large yellow onions, thickly sliced and then quartered

¾ cup dry sherry

2½ cups beef stock

4 medium red potatoes, peeled and quartered

What you'll do

Using a long sharp knife, create a 1½-inch pocket through the center of the roast. You may start on one end and continue on the other, ensuring that the pocket meets in the middle. Carefully stuff the ham pieces into the pocket, using the end of a wooden spoon to get the ham to the other end of the roast.

Season the roast with salt and pepper, place in a nonreactive casserole dish or heavy-duty gallon-size resealable bag, and pour the mojo over it. Refrigerate for at least 6 hours or overnight. (Turn the roast over in the marinade or flip the bag over about halfway through.)

Remove the roast from the marinade, being sure to reserve the marinade, and pat dry.

Heat the olive oil in a medium or large Dutch oven over medium heat. Once the oil is hot and slightly smoking, place the roast in the pot and sear on all sides. Remove the roast from the pot and set aside.

Add the onions to the pot and cook for 3 to 4 minutes, until slightly translucent. Add the stock, bay leaf, oregano, reserved marinade, and sherry to the pot and stir well. Place the roast back in the pot, bring the stock to a boil over medium-high heat, then reduce the heat to low/simmer, cover, and cook for 2 hours, turning the roast over once during the cooking process.

Add the potatoes to the pot and continue cooking, covered, for an additional 30 to 40 minutes, until the potatoes are very tender. You may add additional stock or water if necessary.

Remove the roast from the pot and allow to rest for 8 to 10 minutes. Bring the sauce and potatoes to a low boil and cook, uncovered, for 4 to 5 minutes so that the sauce thickens a bit. Add salt and pepper to taste. Slice the roast into 1½ to 2-inch slices and arrange on a platter with potatoes. Pour the sauce over them. Serve immediately.

Store leftovers covered in the refrigerator for up to 3 days.

Note: For a keto-friendly alternative, substitute parsnips for potatoes. Incorporate into the recipe in the same manner as the potatoes. Parsnips will need an additional 10 minutes to become tender so allow for extra cook time.

keto frien ALTERN

Oxtail Stew

The literal translation of the name of this dish is *Tail on Fire*. As you can imagine, it was another one of those Cuban delicacies I avoided at all costs as a child. I must say, though, I have since developed a certain appreciation for this dish. This recipe results in tender, fall off the bone meat in a rich wine gravy.

gluten free

keto friendly

What you'll need

3 pounds oxtails, trimmed of all visible fat and cut into 2-inch pieces

Salt and pepper

All-purpose flour, for dredging

⅓ cup olive oil

4 garlic cloves, minced

2 cups onion, diced

2 cups green bell pepper, diced

1½ cups potatoes, cut into 2-inch dice

3 tablespoons tomato paste

1 cup canned tomato sauce

1 cup dry red wine

¼ vino seco (dry white cooking wine)

2 cups low-sodium beef stock

1 bay leaf

½ cup parsley chopped

1 teaspoon red wine vinegar

1 teaspoon salt

½ teaspoon black pepper

½ teaspoon ground oregano

½ teaspoon ground cumin

Arroz Blanco (White Rice; page 70), for serving

Plátanitos Maduros (Fried Sweet Plantains; page 122), for serving

What you'll do

Season the oxtails with salt and pepper, dredge them lightly in flour, and set them aside.

Heat the olive oil in a large heavy-bottomed pot over medium-high heat. Add the oxtails in small batches and sear them on all sides. Transfer the seared oxtails to a plate and set them aside.

Reduce the heat to medium and add the garlic, onion, and bell pepper. Sauté for 5 to 7 minutes, until the vegetables are tender. Add the tomato paste and tomato sauce and continue cooking for another 5 minutes. Add the wine, *vino seco,* stock, bay leaf, oregano, cumin, salt, pepper, and vinegar and increase the heat to medium-high. Bring the soup to a slow boil. Add the oxtails, reduce the heat to low, cover the pot, and let the soup simmer for 2 hours.

Add the potatoes and the parsley and continue cooking, covered, for an additional 45 minutes to 1 hour, until the meat is falling off the bones. Taste the soup and adjust the seasonings, if necessary. Remove and discard the bay leaf.

Serve with white rice and fried sweet plantains.

Roast Chicken

This simple dish is a joy to make because it is effortless and fills your home with the undeniable aroma of home cookin'. Every cookbook should have a great roast chicken recipe and this one has that Cuban flavor to make it extra special.

What you'll need

1½ cups sour orange juice (from about 6 oranges) or a mixture of equal parts lime juice and orange juice (reserve the squeezed half of 1 orange)

8 garlic cloves, minced

Salt and pepper

1 (5- to 7-pound) chicken

1 tablespoon sweet paprika

1 teaspoon dried oregano leaves

4 tablespoons (½ stick) salted butter

2 medium sweet onions, 1 peeled and left whole, and 1 quartered

1 bay leaf

4 large carrots, peeled, cut in half lengthwise, then cut in half crosswise

4 medium red potatoes, peeled and cut into 2- to 3-inch pieces

¾ cup dry white wine

¼ cup olive oil

1 cup chicken stock

What you'll do

Combine the orange juice, garlic, and salt and pepper to taste in a bowl.

Season the chicken generously with paprika, oregano, and salt and pepper. Place the chicken, breast-side down, in a large bowl. Pour the orange juice marinade over the chicken, cover it tightly with plastic wrap, and refrigerate for at least 8 hours or overnight.

Preheat the oven to 375°F. Lightly coat a large roasting pan with olive oil.

Remove the chicken from the marinade, reserving the marinade, and place it breast-side up in the roasting pan. Pat the top of the chicken dry with a paper towel and rub the top and sides of the chicken with 2 table-spoons of the butter. Put the reserved orange half inside the cavity of the chicken, along with the whole peeled onion and the bay leaf. Arrange the quartered onion, carrots, and potatoes around the chicken.

Roast the chicken for 1½ to 2 hours, depending on the size of the chicken (allow 20 minutes per pound). You may cover the pan very loosely with foil for the first hour of roasting to prevent the breast from drying out, but be sure to remove the foil during the last hour so the skin browns evenly. Allow the chicken to rest for at least 15 minutes before carving.

Pour the marinade into a large saucepan and bring it to a boil. Add the wine, olive oil, and stock and continue boiling for 10 to 15 minutes or until the marinade is reduced by half and is slightly thickened. Add the 2 remaining table-spoons of butter, stirring to melt and combine it, as this will act as a thickening agent. Add salt and pepper to taste and serve the gravy alongside the cooked chicken.

Note: For a keto-friendly alternative, substitute parsnips for the potatoes. Parsnips will need an additional 10 minutes to become tender. Omit the carrots.

keto frien ALTERN

Cuban-Style Fried Chicken

Fried chicken is delicious, any way you slice it. Cuban fried chicken is of course even better. The mojo marinade imparts a tanginess that you usually get from buttermilk in Southern-style fried chicken.

This recipe requires you to cut a whole fryer chicken into eight pieces. If you are like me—averse to wrestling with uncooked chicken—you can buy a whole chicken already cut into eight pieces at most grocery stores.

What you'll need

1 cup sour orange juice (from about 4 oranges) or a mixture of equal parts lime and orange juice

6 garlic cloves, minced

1 tablespoon plus 1 teaspoon salt

1 teaspoon black pepper

1 (5- to 7-pound) fryer chicken, cut into 8 pieces

4 cups corn oil

2 cups all-purpose flour

1 tablespoon sweet or smoked paprika

½ teaspoon dried oregano leaves

1 teaspoon onion powder

4 large eggs, beaten

What you'll do

Combine the orange juice, garlic, 1 tablespoon of the salt, and ½ teaspoon of the pepper in a large bowl.

Arrange the chicken in a large glass baking pan, pour the orange juice mixture over it, cover with plastic wrap, and refrigerate for at least 8 hours, preferably overnight. Turn the chicken once during the marinating process.

Remove the chicken from the marinade and discard the marinade. Pat the chicken dry with a paper towel.

Heat the oil to about 375°F in a large, deep cast iron skillet over medium-high heat.

Combine the flour, 1 teaspoon of the salt, ½ teaspoon of the pepper, the paprika, oregano, and onion powder in a large bowl and mix well. Dredge each piece of chicken lightly in the flour, then in the beaten eggs, and again in the flour, making sure the chicken is completely coated.

Add four pieces of chicken to the oil and fry them on one side for 8 to 10 minutes, until they turn medium brown on the cooking side. If the chicken is browning too rapidly, reduce the heat slightly. Turn the chicken over and cook for 4 to 5 minutes. Transfer the chicken to drain on a wire rack placed over paper towels or brown paper bags. Bring the oil back up to 375°F and fry and drain the remaining pieces of chicken in the same manner. Let the chicken cool slightly before serving (this also enhances the crispiness).

Chicken Fricassee

This dish is another of the many sofrito-based, one-dish wonders that Cubans enjoy. This is also great the day after it's cooked, making for fantastic leftovers. While the traditional recipe calls for a whole chicken, cut up, my family prefers white meat, so I make this with six large, bone-in chicken breasts. You can do either.

What you'll need

½ cup olive oil

6 large chicken breasts, bone-in and skinless, or 1 (5- to 7-pound) whole fryer chicken, cut into 8 pieces

1 tablespoon salt

1 teaspoon black pepper

4 garlic cloves, minced

1 large onion, chopped

1 medium green bell pepper, chopped

2 cups canned tomato sauce

1 cup chicken stock

½ cup *vino seco* (dry white cooking wine)

1 bay leaf

1 teaspoon dried oregano leaves

1 teaspoon sweet paprika

4 medium red potatoes, peeled and cut into 2- to 3-inch pieces

½ cup pimento-stuffed olives

Arroz Blanco (White Rice; page 70), for serving

Plátanitos Maduros (Fried Sweet Plantains; page 122), for serving

What you'll do

Heat half of the olive oil in a large heavy pot over medium-high heat.

Season the chicken with the salt and pepper, then add it to the pot and sear it for 4 to 5 minutes, until the outside of the chicken pieces turns light golden brown. Transfer the chicken to a plate and set aside.

Heat the remaining olive oil in the pot. Add the garlic, onion, and green pepper, and sauté for 10 to 12 minutes, until the onion caramelizes slightly. Add the tomato sauce, stock, *vino seco*, bay leaf, oregano, and paprika and bring to a boil. Add the chicken and potatoes and reduce the heat to low. Cover the pot and cook for 1 hour.

Store leftovers, covered, in the refrigerator for up to 3 days.

Add the olives and stir well. Taste and adjust the seasonings, if necessary. Remove and discard the bay leaf.

Serve with white rice and fried sweet plantains.

Thanksgiving Day Turkey with Ham Stuffing

Cubans don't celebrate Thanksgiving in Cuba, but here *en el exilio* (in exile), we have taken on the American culinary tradition and made it our own. We call it *Sansgivin* (*Thanksgiving* in broken English), and we feel very American partaking in this holiday. I suspect many Cubans do not really understand the whole pilgrim-and-Indian concept, although some will feign vast knowledge about the first Thanksgiving. I have witnessed grandfathers giving long—partially accurate, partially fabricated, and very humorous—dissertations to their grandchildren about *Sansgivin*. When the story starts with a pilgrim named Pepe, you know you're in trouble.

Turkey, or *el pavo*, is a once-a-year thing for Cubans, and how it is prepared is open to interpretation. We are funny about turkey, with each family handling it in its own special way. For example, some Cuban families insist on being true to tradition and try to make an "Americanized" bird. This is always a disaster. You see, Cubans generally don't cook with spices like sage and rosemary, so when they use them . . . well, they overuse them! So, the turkey ends up tasting a little like perfume! Then there are those who get upset when the turkey actually ends up tasting like turkey, despite the fact that they desperately attempted to make it taste like roast pork!

Then there is the Cuban take on what should be served alongside the bird on Thanksgiving. There may be some mashed potatoes, but nine times out of ten, there is rice and beans and of course, *una pierna* (a leg of pork). You see, Cubans can't live without pork. It's not enough that we always roast an entire pig on Christmas Eve. We need pork at Thanksgiving, as well. As a matter of fact, even our stuffing is made with pork—see recipe below. This is no dry box stuffing, but rather a meal in itself. It has flavors of nutmeg, garlic, and sherry and is studded with raisins and slivered almonds. I like to lightly roast the almonds in the toaster oven at 300°F for five minutes before adding them to the stuffing. The crunchiness adds a nice texture to the dish.

What you'll need

Turkey

1 (14- to 16-pound) turkey

Salt and pepper

½ cup olive oil

2½ to 3 cups sour orange juice (from about 10 oranges) or a mixture of equal parts lime juice and orange juice

1 cup chicken stock

12 garlic cloves, minced

1 large onion, diced

1 tablespoon sweet paprika

1 teaspoon dried oregano leaves

1 teaspoon ground cumin

¼-pound (1 stick) salted butter

Stuffing

¼-pound (1 stick) salted butter, plus more as needed

1 large onion, chopped

3 garlic cloves, minced

1½ pounds ground sweet or honey-baked ham

1 (8-ounce) package cream cheese, softened

½ cup *vino seco* (dry white cooking wine)

1 loaf white sandwich bread, torn into bite-sized pieces

1 teaspoon ground nutmeg

1 teaspoon salt

½ teaspoon white pepper

1 cup heavy cream

¾ cup slivered almonds

¾ cup raisins

What you'll do

To make the turkey, season it generously with salt and pepper, including the inside of the cavity. Place the turkey, breast-side down, inside a container or resealable plastic bag large enough to accommodate it overnight in the refrigerator. You may use a roasting pan if it is nonreactive and deep enough to hold the marinade.

Combine the oil, orange juice, stock, garlic, onion, paprika, oregano, and cumin in a large bowl. Carefully pour the marinade over the turkey, cover it with plastic wrap, and refrigerate it overnight.

The next morning (at least 10 hours before serving), remove the turkey and the stick of butter from the refrigerator and let them warm to room temperature.

Meanwhile, prepare the stuffing. Preheat the oven to 350°F. Butter a large rectangular casserole dish.

Melt the butter in a large pot over medium heat. Add the onion and garlic and sauté for 5 to 7 minutes, until the onion softens. Add the ham, cream cheese, and *vino seco* and cook for

10 minutes, stirring frequently, until the ingredients are fully incorporated. Set aside.

Place the bread in a large bowl. Combine the nutmeg, salt, pepper, and cream in a small bowl and pour the mixture over the bread. Toss to combine. Add the almonds and raisins and toss again. Add the ham mixture and mix well. Pour the bread mixture into the prepared casserole dish, cover it with foil, and bake for 1 hour, removing the foil after 30 minutes. Let the stuffing cool to room temperature.

Preheat the oven to 400°F.

Remove the turkey from the marinade (discard the marinade) and place it in a roasting pan. Rub the butter over the entire turkey, massaging it well. Use your fingers to gently separate the skin from the meat around the breastbone, and rub some butter into the flesh, as well. Stuff the cavity of the turkey with the stuffing.

Roast the turkey for 10 minutes. Reduce the oven temperature to 325°F, loosely cover the bird with foil, and roast for 3 hours, basting every half hour or so. Remove the foil, raise temperature to 350 degrees and continue roasting for another hour, depending on the size of your turkey. A good rule of thumb is 20 minutes per pound. The turkey and stuffing will both be cooked when they reach 165°F when tested with a cooking thermometer.

Let the turkey rest for 20 to 25 minutes before carving.

Store leftovers, covered, in the refrigerator for up to 3 days.

Málaga-Style Eggs

Serves 6

People rarely think of eggs as a dinner dish, but they really are a great high-protein option. *Huevos a la Malaguena* originated in Spain and are similar to French coddled eggs. The eggs are served on top of savory sofrito, which provides an unexpected burst of flavor. The addition of ham and shrimp complete the meal with lots of added protein. This dish is as elegant as it is delicious. It also makes a great brunch dish.

gluten free

What you'll need

18 small shrimp

¼ cup olive oil

1 medium onion, chopped

2 garlic cloves, minced

1 small green bell pepper, chopped

1½ cups canned tomato sauce

1 bay leaf

1 teaspoon salt, plus more as needed

½ teaspoon black pepper, plus more as needed

½ teaspoon sweet or smoked paprika

½ cup *vino seco* (dry white cooking wine)

12 large eggs

6 tablespoons salted butter, melted

½ pound Serrano ham, cut into thin strips

1 cup canned asparagus tips

½ cup canned peas

2 tablespoons chopped fresh parsley

What you'll do

Preheat the oven to 350°F.

Bring 3 cups of lightly salted water to a boil in a large pan. Add the shrimp and boil for 2 to 3 minutes, until the shrimp are opaque. Drain the shrimp and set them aside to cool. Peel and devein the shrimp.

Heat the olive oil in a medium-sized frying pan over medium heat. Add the onion, garlic, and bell pepper and sauté for 5 to 7 minutes, until the vegetables are soft. Add the tomato sauce, bay leaf, salt, black pepper, paprika, and *vino seco*. Reduce the heat to low, cover the pan, and let the sauce simmer for 10 to 15 minutes, until the sauce thickens slightly. Remove and discard the bay leaf. Divide the mixture evenly among six 6-ounce ramekins.

Carefully break 2 eggs into each ramekin and drizzle with 1 tablespoon melted butter. Layer each dish evenly with ham, shrimp, asparagus, and peas. Place the ramekins on a baking sheet and bake for 12 to 14 minutes, until the egg whites are set (completely white). Sprinkle with parsley and salt and pepper to taste.

Cod in Spicy Tomato Sauce

pescatarian

gluten free

My mom used to make this dish every year on Good Friday, the Friday preceding Easter Sunday. It is one of those childhood traditions I remember fondly. Most Cubans have their own interpretation of this unique and tasty dish that originated in Spain. The flavor is wonderful—the tanginess of the tomato sauce coupled with the delicate fish is a delectable combination.

Get started on this recipe at least a day in advance, because you'll have to soak your salt cod for at least twelve hours before cooking it.

What you'll need

1½ pounds salt cod

1 cup olive oil

½ cup all-purpose flour

5 garlic cloves, minced

2 large onions, chopped

1 large green bell pepper, chopped

3 cups canned tomato sauce

½ cup *vino seco* (dry white cooking wine)

2 bay leaves

2 tablespoons sweet paprika

1 teaspoon salt

½ teaspoon white pepper

4 medium to large red potatoes, cut into 2-inch cubes

1 (2-foot) loaf Cuban bread

6 hard-boiled eggs, sliced lengthwise, for garnish

½ cup pimentos, for garnish

½ cup peas, for garnish

1 tablespoon Tabasco sauce, for garnish

Arroz Blanco (White Rice; page 70), for serving

What you'll do

Place the cod in a large bowl and add cool water to cover. Let the cod soak at room temperature for 10 to 12 hours, changing the water every 1 to 2 hours.

Drain the cod and put it in a large pot. Fill the pot three-quarters full of water and bring to a boil. Boil uncovered for 5 to 10 minutes, then reduce the heat to low, cover the pot, and cook for 10 minutes. Reserve 2 cups of the cod cooking water, then drain the cod, discarding the remaining water. Set the cod aside to cool completely.

Heat ¼ cup of the olive oil in a large frying pan over medium-high heat. Cut the cod into large (2- to 3-inch) chunks; remove any bones. Lightly dredge the pieces in the flour and shake off any excess. Carefully place the fish in the hot oil and fry it for 2 to 3 minutes per side, until it turns a light golden color. Transfer the fish to a paper towel–lined plate and set aside.

In the same pot used to boil the cod, heat ½ cup of the olive oil over medium heat. Add the garlic, onions, and bell pepper, and sauté for 10 to 12 minutes, until the vegetables soften and the onion and garlic attain a light golden hue. Add the tomato sauce, *vino seco*, bay leaves, paprika, salt, and black pepper. Raise the heat to high and bring the mixture to a boil, stirring frequently. Let the mixture boil for 3 to 5 minutes, reduce the heat to low, add the potatoes and the reserved cooking liquid,

and cover. Cook for 25 to 30 minutes, until the potatoes are fork-tender. Add the cod and stir, incorporating it completely into the sauce.

In the pan used to fry the cod, heat the remaining ¼ cup olive oil over medium-high heat. Cut the bread into 1½- to 2-inch-thick slices and add to the hot oil. Carefully fry the bread for about 1 minute on each side, until golden brown.

To serve, spoon the fish stew onto a plate and garnish with hard-boiled eggs, pimentos, peas, and Tabasco sauce. Serve with hot, fluffy, white rice and the fried bread.

Note: For a keto-friendly alternative, substitute parsnips for the potatoes. Incorporate into the recipe in the same manner as the potatoes. Parsnips will need an additional 10 minutes to become tender so allow for extra cooking time.

Shrimp in Garlic Sauce

Serves 6 to 8

pescatarian

This dish was definitely my dad's favorite. He never tired of eating it. Many years ago, on our first trip to Spain, I eagerly ordered the *Gambas al Ajillo,* as they refer to this dish there. I was horrified when the waiter brought a small, sizzling clay pot overflowing with humongous, unpeeled shrimp, heads and feet still intact. I was sixteen years old at the time and, frankly, could not bear to look at them. Now I understand that leaving both the shells and heads on shrimp makes this dish more authentic and enhances the flavor.

What you'll need

4 tablespoons (½ stick) salted butter

2 pounds medium shrimp, peeled and deveined, tails on

¾ cup olive oil

1 small yellow onion, diced

15 garlic cloves, minced

1 cup shrimp, fish, or vegetable stock, plus more as needed

½ cup dry white wine

Juice of 1 large lime

2 teaspoons salt

½ teaspoon white pepper

1 teaspoon all-purpose flour

¼ cup minced fresh parsley

Arroz Blanco (White Rice; page 70) or *Arroz Amarillo* (Yellow Rice; page 77), for serving

What you'll do

In a heavy pot, heat 2 tablespoons of the butter over medium heat. Once the butter begins to turn golden brown, add half of the shrimp and quickly sear them (you may have to raise the heat). Transfer the shrimp to a plate and repeat with the remaining butter and shrimp.

In the same pot, heat the olive oil over medium heat. Add the onion and garlic and sauté for 5 to 7 minutes, until both are soft. Add the stock, wine, lime juice, salt, and pepper and bring to a boil. Reduce the heat to low, cover the pot, and cook for 15 to 20 minutes. You may need to add extra stock if the sauce evaporated too quickly, but not more than ¼ cup.

Measure out ½ cup of the hot liquid and place it in a medium-sized bowl. Add the flour and whisk until smooth. Add the flour mixture to the pot and stir until the sauce thickens to the consistency of light syrup. Add the shrimp and the parsley and stir, incorporating all the ingredients completely. Cook for 5 to 7 minutes. Do not overcook the shrimp, or they will be tough.

Serve with white or yellow rice.

Store leftovers, covered, in the refrigerator for up to 2 days.

Note: For a gluten-free, keto-friendly alternative, substitute almond flour for the all-purpose flour (1:1 ratio).

gluten free
ALTERNATE

keto friendly
ALTERNATE

Camarones Enchilados

Shrimp Creole

This shrimp dish is quite typical of Cuban cookery because the shrimp is slowly simmered in sofrito, the tomato-based seasoning that is used to prepare many Cuban dishes. Because shrimp is so delicately flavored, the sauce really penetrates them, both in flavor and color, making the dish as vibrant and colorful as it is delectable.

pescatarian

gluten free

What you'll need

⅓ cup olive oil

4 garlic cloves, minced

1 large onion, diced

1 medium green bell pepper, diced

1½ cups canned tomato sauce

½ cup *vino seco* (dry white cooking wine)

½ cup fish vegetable stock

1 bay leaf

1 teaspoon salt

1 teaspoon black pepper

1 teaspoon sweet or smoked paprika

½ teaspoon dried oregano leaves

2 pounds medium shrimp, peeled and deveined

What you'll need

Heat the olive oil in a large, heavy pot over medium-high heat. Add the garlic, onion, and bell pepper and sauté for 5 to 10 minutes, until the vegetables are soft. Add the tomato sauce, *vino seco,* stock, bay leaf, salt, black pepper, paprika, and oregano and bring to a boil. Cover the pot, reduce the heat to low, and simmer for 30 to 40 minutes. Taste the sauce and adjust the seasonings, if necessary.

Raise the heat and bring the sauce to a boil again. Add the shrimp and cook, stirring frequently, for 5 to 10 minutes, until they turn pink. Watch them carefully—it is important not to overcook the shrimp, as this really toughens them. Remove the pot from the heat and let the shrimp sit for a few minutes in the sauce to allow the flavors to fully penetrate them. Remove and discard the bay leaf.

Variation: *Langosta Enchilada*

(Lobster Creole)

This dish is prepared in exactly the same manner as Camarones Enchilados. The only difference is that 6 or 7 medium fresh lobster tails are substituted for the shrimp. To prepare them, cut the tails (shell on), widthwise, into 2-to-3-inch pieces. Add the lobsters to the sauce (with the shell still attached) when the recipe directs you to add the shrimp, and simmer for 15 to 20 minutes, until the meat is completely opaque. Like shrimp, lobster becomes tough and rubbery when it is overcooked, so watch it carefully!

Note: To make the recipe more keto friendly, substitute sugar-free tomato sauce for tomato sauce.

keto friendly
ALTERNATE

Lobster in Cream Sauce

This dish is unlike anything else you've encountered in this book so far. It is creamy and decadent and oh so rich—quite different from the savory, tomato-based dishes that abound in this cookbook. I love making this dish for dinner parties because it is so elegant. Also, it can be made ahead of time and baked right before serving, making it perfect for entertaining.

pescatarian

What you'll need

¼ pound (1 stick) salted butter, plus more as needed

3 pounds lobster meat, coarsely chopped into ½- to ¾-inch pieces (about 3 cups)

1 tablespoon fresh lemon juice

3 tablespoons *vino seco* (dry white cooking wine)

1 cup whole milk

1 cup half-and-half

⅓ cup all-purpose flour

3 large egg yolks

1 tablespoon Worcestershire sauce

½ teaspoon ground nutmeg

½ teaspoon sweet or smoked paprika

1 teaspoon salt

½ teaspoon white pepper

½ cup breadcrumbs

What you'll do

Heat 4 tablespoons of the butter in a large frying pan over medium-high heat. Add the lobster meat, lemon juice, and *vino seco* and sauté until the lobster is opaque, about 5 minutes. Set aside.

Melt the remaining 4 tablespoons butter. Combine 3 tablespoons of the melted butter, the milk, half-and-half, flour, egg yolks, Worcestershire sauce, nutmeg, paprika, salt, and pepper in a blender or food processor and blend just until fully combined. Do not over blend. Pour the mixture into a large saucepan and cook over medium-low heat, whisking continuously, until the sauce thickens and boils. Reduce the heat to low.

Add the lobster to the pan and stir well so the meat is completely incorporated into the sauce. Taste and adjust the seasonings, if necessary.

Preheat the broiler. Lightly butter a 2-quart casserole or gratin dish or spray it with non-stick cooking spray.

Combine the breadcrumbs with the remaining tablespoon of melted butter in a small bowl and mix well.

Pour the lobster mixture into the prepared dish and sprinkle the top with the breadcrumb mixture. Place the casserole under the broiler for 3 to 5 minutes, until the breadcrumbs turn golden brown.

Variation: *Camarones a la Crema*
(Shrimp in Cream Sauce)

A nice variation of Colas de Langosta a la Crema can be made with shrimp. It makes a wonderful and elegant main course served with Arroz Amarillo (Yellow Rice; page 77), or an equally delicious appetizer served alongside garlic bread. Instead of lobster, use 2 pounds medium (21 to 30 per pound) shrimp, peeled and deveined, and cook as directed above.

Fish in Parsley Garlic Sauce

pescatarian

This is another great dish to serve at dinner parties. You can even make it ahead of time and just warm it up when your guests arrive. There are many variations to the preparation of this dish. Some recipes call for combining the raw fish fillets with the garlic-parsley sauce and then baking it. Other recipes instruct you to cook the fish first, then pour the sauce over it right before serving. My recipe calls for lightly floured and seared fillets that are then baked in the parsley sauce. It's a little more work but well worth it. The light golden color and flavor the searing imparts to the fish makes a huge difference. I also recommend hand chopping the parsley instead of using a food processor, so it will retain its vibrant green color.

What you'll need

6 (6- to 8-ounce) red snapper fillets or other firm-fleshed white fish

2½ teaspoons salt

1 teaspoon white pepper

Juice of 2 limes

½ cup olive oil, plus more as needed

¼ cup all-purpose flour

½ teaspoon sweet or smoked paprika

1½ cups chopped fresh parsley

½ cup diced sweet onion (like Vidalia)

3 tablespoon red wine vinegar

½ teaspoon sugar

2 tablespoons salted butter

8 garlic cloves, minced

1 cup dry white wine

What you'll do

Season the fish with 1 teaspoon of the salt and ½ teaspoon of the pepper and marinate with the lime juice in a nonreactive dish for 30 minutes to 1 hour.

Preheat the oven to 425°F.

Heat half the olive oil in a large sauté pan over medium-high heat. Combine the flour and the paprika in a shallow platter. Dredge the fish fillets in the flour mixture, add them to the pan, and sear for 2 minutes per side. Remove the fish from the pan and set it aside.

In a large bowl, combine the parsley, onion, vinegar, sugar, and the remaining ¼ cup olive oil, 1½ teaspoons white pepper, and ½ teaspoon salt.

Set the same pan used to sear the fish over medium heat, add the butter and garlic, and lightly sauté for 3 minutes. Add the wine, raise the heat, and bring the mixture to a boil. Allow it to boil for 5 minutes, then reduce the heat to low, add the parsley mixture, and stir well. Cook for 5 minutes.

Lightly coat the bottom of a shallow, non-reactive baking dish with olive oil. Arrange the fillets in the dish so they do not overlap.

Taste the parsley sauce and add salt, if necessary. Pour the sauce over the fish and bake for 10 minutes. Reduce the oven temperature to 375°F. and continue baking for an additional 5 to 10 minutes, until the fish is thoroughly cooked. Remove the fish from the oven and let it sit for 5 to 10 minutes before serving.

SIETE

ON THE SIDE

Ah, the side dish. The mainstay of a Thanksgiving meal is also the highlight of any Cuban spread. Can you imagine *arroz con pollo* (page 78) without *maduros* or *tostones* on the side? Of course not! Cuban side dishes are as important as the main dish. They add crispy texture, a caramelized sweet bite, and dimension and satisfaction to main courses. So don't sleep on those side dishes, people!

Yuca con Mojo Criollo

Yuca with Garlic Sauce

Serves 4

gluten
free

vegan

This is a Christmas Eve (*Noche Buena*) staple at our house, and most other Cuban households. In addition to beans and rice, of course. *Yuca* is a unique and mildly flavored root vegetable that stands up very well to the tangy savory mojo, or garlic sauce. My recipe calls for fresh yuca, but frozen is just as good and easier to find at most markets.

What you'll need

For the Yuca

3 large or 4 medium yuca (about 2 pounds), peeled and cut into 3-inch chunks, or
1 (2.5-pound) bag frozen yuca

Salt

For the Mojo Criollo

½ cup olive oil

10 to 12 garlic cloves, minced

1 medium yellow onion, grated

2 teaspoons salt

½ teaspoon white pepper

¾ cup sour orange juice or a mixture of equal parts lime juice and orange juice

What you'll do

To make the yuca, fill a large pot with water, add the yuca and salt to taste, and bring to a boil. Boil, uncovered, for 5 minutes, then reduce the heat to medium-low and cover. Cook for 45 minutes to 1 hour, until the yuca is fork-tender.

To make the mojo, heat the oil in a medium saucepan over medium-low heat. Add the garlic, onion, salt, and pepper and sauté for 10 to 15 minutes. Remove from the heat and add the orange juice. Set aside to cool to room temperature.

Drain the yuca and serve it hot, with mojo.

French Fried Potatoes

You just won't be able to get enough of these divinely crispy fries, and neither will anyone else, so make sure you have plenty of potatoes on hand.

gluten free

vegan

What you'll need

Sea salt, to taste

2 to 3 cups corn oil

4 to 6 large red potatoes (about 2½ to 3 pounds)

What you'll do

Fill a large bowl with cold water, then stir in 2 tablespoons salt.

In a large, heavy pot over medium-high, heat 3 to 4 inches of oil to 375°F.

While the oil heats, peel the potatoes, then cut them into ¼ inch slices. Place the slices in the cold water. Working with a stack of 3 or 4 potato slices, cut them into thick sticks, about ⅛ inch wide. Return the sticks to the cold water.

Drop a small piece of potato into the oil to see if it is hot enough to begin cooking. If the oil sizzles around the potato, it is ready. You'll be frying the potatoes in batches, so remove one-third of the potatoes from the water and dry them *thoroughly*. Carefully add the potatoes to the oil and fry them for 7 to 10 minutes, until crispy. Make sure to turn the fries frequently to prevent them from sticking together, and keep an eye on them or they will burn. Transfer the fried potatoes to a paper towel–lined plate and sprinkle them generously with salt. Continue with the remaining potatoes.

Serve immediately.

Fried Sweet Plantains

gluten free

vegan

There is nothing much to this recipe, and yet it is somewhat complicated to execute. The cooking is not the difficult part—all you do is peel, slice, and fry. The key is making sure you have the *right plantain*—it must be at the perfect stage of ripeness. My method is not foolproof, but here it is: Ripe plantains are—well, not green. They are yellow and black, but mostly black. Basically, a ripe plantain is a plantain that's past its prime. It becomes darker and softer as it ripens and releases more sugar, ensuring the sweet caramelized deliciousness that is the hallmark of maduros.

What you'll need

2 or 3 large *ripe* (black) plantains

2 to 3 cups corn or vegetable oil

What you'll do

In a large, heavy pot over medium-high heat, heat 2 to 3 inches of oil to 375°F.

Peel the plantains as you would peel bananas. Because they are soft, the skin will come off easily. Slice the plantains diagonally into 1-inch pieces. Carefully place 4 or 5 plantain slices into the hot oil and cook, turning only once, for about 2 to 3 minutes on each side, until golden brown. Transfer the fried plantains to a paper towel–lined plate to drain and continue with the remaining plantains. Serve immediately.

Fried Green Plantains

Serves 6 to 8

For this recipe, green plantains are fried, then flattened, then fried again. Traditionally, *tostones* were flattened with newspaper or a *tostonera,* a special device created specifically for this culinary purpose. I don't use the newspaper for sanitary reasons, and the *tostonera,* in my opinion, is an unnecessary gadget that will just clutter your kitchen. Wax or parchment paper work just as well.

The trickiest thing about making these delicacies is choosing the right variety of plantain. My personal favorite is the Hawaiian plantain, which is shorter and uniformly fatter than its traditional Cuban counterpart. These are not always available at regular supermarkets, but small Hispanic markets usually carry them and they are kind of foolproof. They always come out of the fryer crispy on the outside and tender and delicious on the inside. If, however, you cannot find them, buy really dark green plantains, peel them, and soak them in salted water for 10 to 15 minutes before frying them.

Just be sure to dry the plantains well before frying them to prevent the hot oil from splattering. Remember to serve them with some mojo on the side!

gluten free

vegan

What you'll need

3 cups corn oil

3 Hawaiian plantains or green plantains

Coarse salt

What you'll do

Heat 2 to 3 inches of oil to 375°F in a large, heavy pot over medium heat. Cut about half an inch from both ends of each plantain, then cut each plantain, with the skin on, into 1½- to 2-inch slices. Use your knife to peel the skin off each slice.

Carefully place 4 or 5 plantain slices in the oil; it should be hot enough to bubble around the plantains, but not so vigorously that it begins to add color right away. Fry the plantains for 3 minutes on each side, then transfer them to a paper towel–lined plate to drain and cool slightly. Fry the remaining slices in the same manner, allowing the oil to return to 375°F between batches. Leave the oil over low-medium heat to keep warm for the second stage of frying.

Once you have fried all the slices, start flattening them, beginning with the first batch, which should have cooled by now. Place the plantain slices, one at a time, between two pieces of wax or parchment paper and press down with the heel of your hand, flattening the plantain slices to about ¾ inch thick. Repeat with the remaining slices.

Raise the heat under the oil to medium and let the oil heat to 375°F. Fry the plantains a second time, in batches, for about 2 to 3 minutes on each side, until they are golden and crispy around the edges. Transfer them to a paper towel–lined plate to drain and sprinkle them generously with coarse salt. Serve immediately.

Spanish-Style French Fries

gluten free

vegan

Basically, *papas Españolas* are Spain's answer to the French fry. The difference is in how they are cut. The disc shape of Spanish-style fries creates a unique texture with crispy edges and a tender center. They are particularly good sprinkled with fresh parsley and smoked paprika. Make these in large quantities, because they tend to disappear quickly.

What you'll need

2 to 3 cups canola oil

2 pounds small to medium red potatoes, peeled and cut crosswise into ⅛-inch discs

Coarse salt

Smoked paprika

What you'll do

In a large, heavy-bottomed, cast iron pot, heat 3 inches of oil to 350°F. Add the potatoes in small batches, and fry for 5 to 7 minutes, just until they begin to turn a light golden color. Transfer the fries to a paper towel–lined platter. Allow the oil to come to 350°F and continue with the remaining potatoes.

Just before serving, heat the oil to 375°F and fry the potatoes again, in batches, for 2 to 3 minutes. The second round of frying crisps them up and make them a deeper golden color. Drain over paper towels and sprinkle with coarse salt and paprika.

Mashed Potatoes

Comfort food, anyone? I bet you're wondering what a recipe for mashed potatoes is doing in a Cuban cookbook. Almost every culture has its version of mashed potatoes, and this is a good one.

gluten free

What you'll need

2 pounds Yukon gold potatoes, peeled and cut into 2-inch pieces

4 garlic cloves, peeled

1 cup whole milk, warmed

4 tablespoons salted butter, melted

½ cup heavy cream, warmed

2 teaspoons salt, or more if needed

½ teaspoon white pepper, or more if needed

What you'll do

Bring 2 quarts of water to a boil in a large pot. Add the potatoes and garlic cloves. Reduce the heat to medium and cook the potatoes, partially covered, for 40 to 45 minutes, until they are fork-tender.

Combine the milk, butter, and cream in a bowl.

Drain the potatoes into a colander, remove and discard the garlic cloves, and return the potatoes to the pot. Using a handheld mixer, beat the potatoes until they break apart. Add the milk mixture little by little while still beating. Once all the ingredients are fully incorporated, add the salt and pepper. Taste and adjust the seasonings, if necessary. Serve immediately.

Note: For vegan mashed potatoes, substitute plant-based milk and butter alternatives.

vegan ALTERNATIVE

Fried Chickpeas and Spanish Sausage

I always have the ingredients for *garbanzo frito* in my pantry. It is a simple flavorful dish that can do double and triple duty. For brunch serve with a fried egg on top, as a tapas-style appetizer. For dinner serve with some fluffy white rice and *maduros* alongside.

What you'll need

½ cup olive oil

1 large onion, chopped

4 garlic cloves, minced

½ cup canned tomato sauce

¾ pound Spanish chorizo sausage, cut into ½-inch slices

2 (15.5-ounce) cans chickpeas, drained and rinsed

1 teaspoon salt

½ teaspoon pepper

1 teaspoon sweet or smoked paprika

Arroz Blanco (White Rice; page 70), for serving

What you'll need

Heat the olive oil in a large frying pan over medium heat. Add the onion and garlic and sauté for 5 to 7 minutes, until the onion is translucent. Add the tomato sauce and cook for 5 minutes more. Increase the temperature to medium-high and add the chorizo (you can remove the casings from the chorizo, if you prefer). Stir frequently for about 3 minutes, until the chorizo renders some of its fat. Reduce the temperature to medium, add the chickpeas, salt, pepper, and paprika, and stir, pressing down on the chickpeas with the back of a wooden spoon to break some of them up. Cook for 5 to 7 minutes, until the chickpeas around the edge of the pan turn golden brown. Taste and adjust the seasonings, if necessary. Serve with white rice.

Malanga Purée

Serves 6 to 8

gluten free

When I was little, I knew I was sick when my mother brought me Welch's grape juice and *puré de malanga* on a tray. I have no idea why she brought the grape juice, but the *malanga* is a traditional Cuban healing remedy. *Malanga* is a root vegetable similar to a potato, with a delicious and distinctive flavor. Once I was older, I feigned many an illness just to get some *malanga* purée. To reheat any leftovers, you may need to add a little warmed milk or water to thin it out.

What you'll need

2 pounds *malanga,* peeled and cut into 1-inch pieces

1½ to 2 cups whole milk, warmed

4 tablespoons salted butter, melted

Salt and white pepper

What you'll do

Bring 2 quarts of water to a boil in a large pot. Add the *malanga* and reduce the heat to medium. Cook the *malanga,* partially covered, for 35 to 40 minutes, until it is fork-tender.

Combine the milk and butter in a bowl.

Drain the *malanga* into a colander, then return it to the pot. Using a handheld mixer, beat the *malanga* until it breaks apart. Add the milk mixture little by little while still beating. Once all the ingredients are fully incorporated and the *malanga* is the consistency of mashed potatoes, season it with salt and pepper. Taste and adjust the seasoning, if necessary. Serve immediately.

Note: For a vegan malanga purée, substitute plant-based milk and a butter alternative.

vegan ALTERNATIVE

Sweet Plantain Casserole

gluten free

Any recipe with a name that includes the word *tentación* (temptation) in it, and is made with butter, rum, and brown sugar, *must* be made immediately. This divinely rich plantain casserole makes for a great Thanksgiving side dish. Make sure you use extremely ripe plantains in this recipe—the skins should be black and the flesh should feel mushy when pressed.

What you'll need

3 *very ripe* (black) plantains

4 tablespoons salted butter

½ cup packed light brown sugar

¼ cup dark rum

½ teaspoon salt

½ teaspoon ground nutmeg

½ teaspoon ground cinnamon

What you'll do

Preheat the oven to 350°F. Butter a 13 × 9-inch baking pan.

Peel the plantains and cut them on a diagonal into 2-inch-thick slices. Arrange the plantain slices in a single layer on the bottom of the prepared pan. Set aside.

Heat the butter and brown sugar in a small saucepan over medium heat until the mixture begins to bubble. Reduce the heat to low, then add the rum, salt, nutmeg, and cinnamon. Stir well and pour evenly over the plantains.

Cover the pan with aluminum foil and bake for 15 minutes.

Remove the dish from the oven, remove the foil, and flip the plantain slices over. Cover the dish with foil and bake for another 15 minutes.

Remove the foil and bake for 10 minutes to brown the top. Serve immediately.

Crunchy Manchego Mac and Cheese with Chorizo Serves 6 to 8

No book is complete without a pasta recipe. And while this is not traditional in any way, it is a Latin twist on a traditional all-American recipe. It is a favorite among my family and friends and I'm willing to bet yours will love it too.

What you'll need

1 cup panko breadcrumbs

¼ cup chopped fresh flat-leaf parsley

6 tablespoons salted butter, softened

1½ teaspoon salt, plus more as needed

¼ teaspoon white pepper

1 pound macaroni, penne, or cavatelli pasta

12 ounces Spanish chorizo sausage, casings removed, diced

½ cup finely chopped sweet yellow onion

2 medium shallots, finely chopped

⅓ cup all-purpose flour

2 tablespoons Dijon mustard

½ teaspoon cayenne pepper

5 cups whole milk

8 ounces shredded white cheddar cheese (about 2 cups)

8 ounces shredded Manchego cheese (about 2 cups)

What you'll do

Preheat the oven to 400°F. Bring a large pot of very well salted water to a boil over high heat.

In a small bowl, combine the bread crumbs with the parsley and 1 tablespoon of the butter. Season with ½ teaspoon (or more) salt and ¼ teaspoon white pepper. Mix well.

Add the pasta to the boiling water and cook according to the package directions until al dente. Drain and set aside.

Add 1 tablespoon of the butter to the pot used to cook the pasta, and place over medium-high heat until melted. Add the chorizo and cook until the edges start to brown a bit, approximately 2 to 3 minutes. Remove the chorizo to a bowl and set aside.

Reduce the heat to medium and add the remaining 4 tablespoons butter. Once the butter is melted, add the onion and shallots and cook, stirring occasionally, until softened, about 4 to 5 minutes. Add the flour, 1 teaspoon salt, the mustard, and cayenne pepper and cook, stirring continuously, for 3 minutes or until the flour has darkened a bit.

Heat the milk in a medium saucepan over medium-high heat, but do not boil. Slowly add the hot milk to the flour mixture whisking continuously until the mixture is smooth. Continue cooking for 7 to 8 minutes until thickened.

Add the cheddar and Manchego cheeses and stir until completely melted and the sauce is smooth. Stir in the pasta and chorizo and mix until heated through. Taste and season with salt as needed.

Transfer the mixture to a 13 × 9-inch baking dish and spread into an even layer. Sprinkle with the panko mixture and bake until bubbling around the edges, about 18 to 20 minutes. Serve immediately.

Store leftovers, covered, in the refrigerator for up to 3 days.

OCHO

HAPPY ENDING

Desserts, Cocktails, and Cafecito

I am going to make a very broad statement here. Ready? Here goes . . . no self-respecting Cuban can leave the dinner table without dessert.

Ok, maybe that's a stretch. Truth be told, I am sort of a dessert junkie. I suspect it's genetic. I, for one, blame my mother for this addiction. Back in the day, the fatter the baby, the more beautiful she was. Well, let me tell you, I was gorgeous! Looking back at my baby pictures, I realize how difficult it must have been for me to develop motor skills since I didn't seem to have any wrists. I am not kidding—my upper extremities went from fat arm to fat hand. No evidence of a wrist anywhere.

Cubans eat dessert, period. Something about our food almost requires it. It does not have to be a giant piece of flan. A little sliver of anything sweet will do. It's probably why guava paste and cream cheese or even canned papaya chunks are so popular in Cuban households. They are easy to have on hand. If you really want to indulge (and you should) or are planning a gathering of any kind, your family and friends will be delighted by any of the recipes in this section. Followed by a shot of Cuban coffee, of course!

Caramel Sauce

This is caramel sauce Cuban style! And it is by far the easiest and most delicious sauce you've ever had because it only requires one ingredient. How is that for easy?

What you'll need

1 (14-ounce) can sweetened condensed milk

What you'll do

My preferred method for making *dulce de leche* is the classic in-the-can method. It's quite simple: Place the unopened can of sweetened condensed milk in a large saucepan, add enough water to completely submerge the can, then bring the water to a boil. Lower the heat slightly and keep the water at a low boil for 2 to 3 hours, making sure the water level always stays above the top of the can. *This is very important! If the can is not submerged at all times, it could explode.* The longer it cooks, the thicker and darker the *dulce de leche* will be; after 2 hours, you'll be able to drizzle it; after 3 hours, it will be thick enough to sandwich between cookies. Let the can cool thoroughly before you open it.

Another way of making *dulce de leche* is with a pressure cooker. Although this method is much faster than the method above, the idea of putting a sealed can that is under pressure inside a pressure cooker that is under pressure is not my cup of tea! But try it if you're brave: Place the can in the pressure cooker and submerge it completely in water. Following the manufacturer's directions, cook it for 20 to 30 minutes.

The fastest and safest method to make *dulce de leche* is to pour the condensed milk into a small saucepan and simmer it over low heat, stirring continuously, until the milk achieves the consistency and color you desire.

Store in an airtight container in the refrigerator for up to 7 days.

Natilla

Vanilla Custard

Serves 8

Natilla is basically Cuban crème brûlée or a rich vanilla pudding. Most places serve traditional *natilla* with a light sprinkling of cinnamon. However, you can take out your handy dandy kitchen torch, caramelize some sugar on top, and call it *crema a la Catalana*. I would not use low-fat milk in this recipe. It will affect both the taste and the consistency. So just splurge on whole milk.

vegetarian

What you'll need

4 cups whole milk

8 large egg yolks

1½ cups sugar

¼ teaspoon salt

¼ cup cornstarch

2 teaspoons pure vanilla extract

Ground cinnamon, for sprinkling

What you'll do

Combine the milk, egg yolks, sugar, salt, and cornstarch in a large bowl. Stir well, until the sugar is completely dissolved. Strain the mixture through a fine sieve into a heavy saucepan. Stir in the vanilla and set the pan over medium heat. Cook the mixture, stirring continuously with a whisk or wooden spoon until it begins to boil, then reduce the heat to medium-low and cook until the mixture thickens, about 15 to 20 minutes. (My mother insists on the wooden spoon. She also insists the spoon must make a noise like this: "*pakata pakata pakata . . .*" That's the noise it makes when it hits the sides of the saucepan; yeah, don't ask!).

Pour the custard into 8 individual ramekins and set aside to cool to room temperature. Cover the ramekins lightly with plastic wrap and refrigerate for at least 1 hour, until the custard sets. Sprinkle with cinnamon immediately before serving.

Store in an airtight container in the refrigerator for 3 to 5 days.

Rice Pudding

gluten free

vegetarian

Cubans adore this decadent, creamy, concoction made with sweetened condensed milk. *Arroz con leche* is a traditional Cuban dessert and it is especially delicious hot from the pot (cook's treat) but is usually served chilled with a sprinkling of cinnamon.

What you'll need

¾ cup short-grain white rice (Valencia or Italian arborio rice)

1 tablespoon salted butter

Half a lime

2 cups whole milk

1 can sweetened condensed milk

½ cup sugar

1 cinnamon stick

¼ teaspoon salt

Ground cinnamon, for finishing

What you'll do

Bring 2 cups of water to boil in a heavy saucepan over medium-high heat. Add the rice and butter and cook, uncovered, for 5 minutes. Reduce the heat to low, cover the pan, and continue cooking for another 15 minutes. Remove from the heat and set aside.

Using a vegetable peeler, carefully peel away the lime zest, green part only, from the lime. You will be removing this from the pudding later on, so make sure you create larger peelings.

In a large bowl, combine the lime zest, milk, condensed milk, sugar, cinnamon stick, and salt.

Use a fork to fluff up the rice, making sure it is not stuck to the bottom of the pot. Pour in the milk mixture and return the pan to the stove. Cook over low heat, stirring frequently, for 40 to 45 minutes, until the pudding thickens. Set aside to cool to room temperature, then refrigerate for at least 1 hour, until the pudding sets.

To serve, remove the cinnamon stick and lime zest and sprinkle with a generous amount of cinnamon.

Store in an airtight container in the refrigerator for up to 5 days.

Cheesecake de Guayaba

Guava Cheesecake

You and I both know that no one ever made cheesecake in Cuba. It is by no means an authentic and traditional Cuban dessert, but this recipe is so good, I had to include it. Guava cheesecake has become increasingly popular and is served at many restaurants today. This recipe creates something completely unlike the crumbly, dry cheesecake topped with a thin layer of guava puree served at many of these establishments. This one is rich, creamy, and pink. The fruit purée is actually incorporated into the dense cheese batter, so it is truly *guava* cheesecake.

vegetarian

You can find canned or jarred guava marmalade at most supermarkets in the Hispanic food section.

What you'll need

1½ cups graham cracker crumbs (about 12 graham crackers)

¾ cup sugar

4 tablespoons salted butter, at room temperature

16 ounces full-fat cream cheese

1 tablespoon pure vanilla extract

1½ cups half-and-half

2 cups guava marmalade (1 16-ounce jar)

What you'll do

Preheat the oven to 400°F.

Combine the graham cracker crumbs, ¼ cup of the sugar, and the butter in a bowl. Firmly press the graham cracker mixture into the bottom of an 8- or 9-inch springform pan and about 1 inch up the sides. Place the pan on a baking sheet and bake the crust for 10 minutes. Set aside to cool while you prepare the filling. Leave the oven set to 400°F.

In a large bowl, beat the cream cheese, vanilla, and remaining ½ cup sugar with an electric hand mixer until fluffy. Gradually add the half-and-half and mix until the batter is thin and free of lumps. Beat in 1 cup of the guava marmalade. Pour the filling into the cooled pie crust and bake for 15 minutes. Reduce the heat to 300°F and bake for 1 hour 15 minutes more. Turn off the heat and allow the cheesecake to cool in the oven with the oven door partially open.

Once the cheesecake has reached room temperature, cover it with plastic wrap and refrigerate for at least 6 hours, preferably overnight.

Spread the remaining cup of guava marmalade over the top of the cheesecake before serving.

Store in an airtight container in the refrigerator for up to 5 days.

My Mom's Famous Butter Pound Cake

vegetarian

My daughters have always called my mother Tita, which is short for *abuelita* ("grandmother" in Spanish). My mother's pound cake is the best, hands down! It was the base for all my elaborate childhood birthday cakes, but it is probably best when eaten plain or with a light dusting of confectioners' sugar. The batter is even better—my daughters insist I leave them some whenever I make this cake. I warn them about uncooked eggs and salmonella, but I lose all credibility as soon as I get caught licking the spoon.

What you'll need

½ pound (2 sticks) salted butter, softened

2 cups sugar

4 large eggs

1 tablespoon vanilla extract

1 cup whole milk

3 cups self-rising flour, sifted

¼ cup confectioners' sugar, for dusting

What you'll do

Preheat the oven to 350°F. Grease and flour two round 9-inch cake pans, a loaf pan, or a 13 × 9-inch baking pan.

In a large mixing bowl, beat together the butter and sugar with an electric mixer on medium-high speed until creamy. Add the eggs, one at a time, beating well after each addition.

Combine the vanilla and milk in a bowl, then add the mixture gradually to the butter mixture. Add the flour ½ cup at a time and continue beating until it is fully incorporated. Do not over beat.

Pour the batter into the prepared pan(s) and bake for 35 to 45 minutes, until a toothpick inserted in the center of the cake comes out clean. Set aside to cool completely.

Just before serving, dust the cake with confectioners' sugar.

Meringue Cookies

I've always considered *merenguitos* to be a healthier version of a cookie. My girls and I love them. Granted they have a ton of sugar but at least they don't contain flour or fat. A *merenguito* is basically a crispy sweet egg white omelet! Ok, maybe that's a stretch. For fancier *merenguitos*, pipe them onto parchment paper with a star-tipped cake decorating bag.

gluten free

vegetarian

What you'll need

3 large egg whites

⅛ teaspoon cream of tartar

1 cup sugar

What you'll do

Preheat the oven to 350°F. Line 2 baking sheets with parchment paper.

Combine the egg whites and cream of tartar in a medium-sized bowl and beat them with an electric hand mixer on medium speed until soft peaks form. Gradually add the sugar, then beat on high speed until the whites are stiff and shiny.

Drop the egg white mixture by rounded table-spoonfuls onto the prepared baking sheets, spacing them 1 inch apart. Bake for 25 minutes, until the cookies are dry. Turn the oven off and allow the *merenguitos* to rest in the oven for at least 12 hours or overnight.

Cuban-Style Bread Pudding

vegetarian

Cuban bread pudding is a little different from the bread pudding that you will find at most restaurants. Ours is served chilled and topped with simple syrup instead of a richer *crème anglaise* or butter rum sauce. Still, as an alternative, I have also included the recipe for an orange-butter rum sauce that I just adore. I think it goes best with a warm bread pudding. This recipe is delicious either way. You can serve the pudding directly from the fridge or the oven.

What you'll need

1 cup whole milk

1 (14-ounce) can sweetened condensed milk

1 (14-ounce) can light fruit cocktail, undrained (perhaps the only time you'll see the word "light" in this book)

1 teaspoon pure vanilla extract

½ teaspoon ground cinnamon

½ cup packed light brown sugar

½ cup sliced almonds, lightly toasted

½ cup raisins

3 tablespoons brandy or amaretto

4 large eggs, beaten

Pinch of salt

1 (2-foot) loaf day-old Cuban bread, torn into 2-inch pieces

6 tablespoons salted butter, melted

What you'll do

Combine the milk, condensed milk, fruit cocktail, vanilla, cinnamon, brown sugar, almonds, raisins, brandy, eggs, and salt in a large bowl and mix until fully incorporated.

In another large bowl, toss the bread with 4 tablespoons of the melted butter.

Use the remaining 2 tablespoons of melted butter to grease a 2-quart Pyrex or glass baking dish.

Pour the milk mixture over the bread and toss well. Allow this mixture to sit for 35 to 45 minutes, until most of the liquid is absorbed by the bread.

Preheat the oven to 350°F.

Pour the bread mixture into the prepared baking pan and bake for 1 to 1½ hours, until the pudding sets.

Serve warm or set aside to cool to room temperature, then refrigerate for 4 hours, or overnight. Top with simple syrup or the orange-butter rum sauce (recipes follow).

For the Simple Syrup

What you'll need

1 cup sugar

Zest from half a lime

1 cinnamon stick

Pinch of salt

What you'll do

Combine the sugar, 1 cup water, the lime zest, cinnamon stick, and salt in a small saucepan and bring the mixture to a boil. Reduce the heat to low and cook until the volume is reduced by half, about 15 to 20 minutes. Remove and discard the cinnamon stick and lime zest and chill before serving.

For the Orange-Butter Rum Sauce

What you'll need

¼ pound (1 stick) salted butter

¼ cup vanilla-flavored rum (Bacardi makes a good one)

½ cup orange juice

2 cups confectioners' sugar

¼ cup heavy cream

What you'll do

Melt the butter in a medium saucepan over low heat. Add the rum and orange juice and bring to a boil. Allow the mixture to boil for 3 to 5 minutes, stirring frequently, in order for the alcohol to evaporate. Watch closely so it doesn't burn.

Remove the sauce from the heat, add the sugar, and whisk or beat it with an electric hand mixer on low speed until no lumps remain. Add the cream in a steady stream, mixing all the while until fully incorporated. Return the sauce to the stovetop and simmer over low heat for 5 minutes. Pour the sauce over the bread pudding while the sauce is still warm.

Store the cooled bread pudding, covered, in the refrigerator for up to 7 days.

Churros have become increasingly popular in recent years, and you can find them at many a restaurant and food court. And while Mexican cuisine has its own version, my favorite are the Spanish-style churros, freshly fried and sprinkled generously with granulated sugar, and then dipped into hot chocolate.

vegetarian

What you'll need

2½ tablespoons sugar, plus ½ to ¾ cup sugar, for sprinkling

½ teaspoon salt

2 tablespoons vegetable oil

1 cup all-purpose flour

2 quarts oil, for frying

What you'll do

Combine 1 cup water, 2½ tablespoons sugar, the salt, and vegetable oil in a small saucepan and place over medium heat. Bring to a boil and then remove from the heat. Add the flour and stir until mixture forms a ball of dough.

Heat the oil for frying in a deep fryer or deep pot to 375°.

Transfer the dough to a sturdy pastry bag fitted with a medium star tip. Working in batches so you don't crowd the fryer, carefully pipe a few 5- to 6-inch strips of dough into the hot oil. Cook until golden, then use a spider or slotted spoon to transfer the churros to paper towels to drain.

Place on a serving platter and sprinkle generously with sugar. Serve with Cuban-style hot chocolate (page 159). Don't forget to dip the churros in the hot chocolate!

Pastelitos de Guayaba y Queso

Guava and Cheese Pastries

Serves 4 to 6

vegetarian

In Miami most people just go to a local bakery to pick up these delicious guava- and cheese-filled pastries along with some other flavors, a few *croquetas,* and the requisite café con leche. But we don't all live in Miami and this recipe is just so easy to make that I had to include it.

What you'll need

1 large egg yolk

1 tablespoon whole milk

All-purpose flour, for dusting

1 (14-ounce) package all-butter puff pastry, thawed

6 ounces guava paste, mashed (see Note)

6 ounces cream cheese, cut into 6 pieces and chilled

Sugar, for sprinkling

What you'll do

Arrange an oven rack in the center of the oven and preheat the oven to 375°. In a small bowl, whisk the egg yolk with the milk.

On a lightly floured work surface, unfold the puff pastry and cut it into 6 squares. Transfer the squares to a parchment paper–lined baking sheet. Cut the guava paste into 6 equal portions and spoon onto one half of each pastry square. Top each portion of guava paste with a piece of the cream cheese. Brush the pastry edges with some of the egg wash. Fold the pastry over the filling to form rectangles and crimp the edges of each pastry with a fork. Refrigerate for 15 minutes, until firm.

Brush the pastries with the remaining egg wash and sprinkle with sugar. Bake in the center of the oven for 30 minutes, rotating the pan from front to back halfway through, until the pastries are golden. Let cool for at least 30 minutes before serving.

Note: Guava paste is firm and solid and usually comes in bars or in a can. You may heat the paste for 2 to 3 minutes in a microwave at 50 percent power to make it easier to mash.

Guava and Cream Cheese Pound Cake with Spiced Rum Glaze   Serves 6 to 8

This is a recipe that I had to include for fear of being boycotted by my family and friends. It's a favorite among my tribe, and frequently what I bring to people's homes when they request that I bring dessert. I'll often pick up a guava and cream cheese ice cream called "Abuela Maria" at Azucar, a popular Miami ice cream shop to serve alongside. As an alternative, a homemade vanilla or French vanilla ice cream like Blue Bell or Haagen Daz's dulce de leche flavor is a perfect complement to this delicious cake.

vegetarian

What you'll need

For the Glaze

¾ cup spiced rum

½ cup granulated sugar

4 tablespoons (½ stick) salted butter

½ cup confectioners' sugar

For the Cake

1½ cups salted butter, softened

1 (8 ounce) package cream cheese, softened

2 cups granulated sugar

6 large eggs

1 tablespoon pure vanilla extract

¾ cup guava marmalade (not jelly)

3 cups all-purpose flour

¼ teaspoon salt

What you'll do

Preheat the oven to 325°F.

To make the glaze, combine the rum, granulated sugar, and butter in a medium saucepan and bring to a boil over medium-high heat. Reduce the heat to low and simmer for 3 to 5 minutes, stirring occasionally until the sugar is completely dissolved and the alcohol has evaporated. Set aside to cool.

To make the cake, cream together the butter and cream cheese using an electric hand mixer or a stand mixer. Gradually add the granulated sugar and beat for 3 to 5 minutes, until fluffy. Add the eggs, one at a time, and beat for another minute.

Add the vanilla and guava marmalade and mix until they are incorporated and the mixture takes on a pinkish hue. Sift the flour and salt together and add gradually to the mixer, beating until incorporated.

Pour the batter into a greased and floured Bundt pan or two loaf pans. Bake the cake in the preheated oven for 1 hour 15 minutes, or until a toothpick inserted in the center comes out clean.

Place a wire rack on top of a large piece of foil or parchment paper to collect any glaze drippings. Place the cake on the lined wire rack and cool for 5 minutes.

Add the confectioners' sugar to the rum glaze and whisk until smooth. Pour the glaze evenly over the cake. Allow to sit for at least 45 minutes before transferring to a cake plate.

Best Flan Ever, Three Ways

Serves 6

This is the quintessential Cuban dessert. You'll find it on every single Cuban restaurant's menu. But not all flan is created equal, and while the ingredients are often similar, the process varies quite a bit. I love a dense, decadent flan without those little air bubbles that, to me, ruin the experience of my spoon carving off a bite of this sweet, creamy caramel-topped delicacy. I've provided you with three versions. All are equally good.

gluten free

vegetarian

Flan de Leche

Traditional Flan

What you'll need

¾ cup sugar

4 large egg yolks

2 large eggs

1 (14-ounce) can sweetened condensed milk

1 (14-ounce) can evaporated milk

2 teaspoons pure vanilla extract

½ teaspoon salt

What you'll do

Preheat the oven to 325°.

Heat ½ cup of the sugar in a small saucepan over medium-low heat for 5 to 7 minutes, stirring occasionally, until the sugar melts and becomes syrupy. Once the syrup begins to turn a light caramel color, pour it into six 4- to 6-inch ramekins.

Place the remaining ¼ cup of sugar, the egg yolks, eggs, condensed milk, evaporated milk, vanilla, and salt in a blender. Blend on medium-high speed until thoroughly combined. Divide the mixture evenly among the ramekins.

Fill a large rectangular baking pan halfway with water. Carefully set the ramekins in the pan, ensuring that no water gets in the ramekins (this water-bath method is crucial, as custard will not set otherwise). Place the pan in the oven and bake for 45 to 50 minutes until the custard is set. Allow the ramekins to cool before transferring them to the refrigerator to chill for a minimum of 4 hours or overnight.

Remove from the refrigerator 30 minutes before serving. When ready to serve, run a thin knife around each ramekin to loosen the custard and invert into individual dessert plates.

Store covered in the refrigerator for up to 7 days.

Flan de Queso

Cream Cheese Flan   Serves 6

What you'll need

1 cup sugar

4 large eggs

2 large egg yolks

1 (14-ounce) can sweetened condensed milk

1 (14-ounce) can evaporated milk

1 teaspoon pure vanilla extract

8 ounces full-fat cream cheese (none of that low-fat stuff), at room temperature

¼ teaspoon salt

What you'll do

Preheat the oven to 325°F.

Heat ½ cup of the sugar in a small saucepan over medium-low heat for 15 to 20 minutes, stirring occasionally, until the sugar melts. Watch it closely so that it does not burn. Once the sugar has completely melted and turned a light caramel color, divide it evenly among six 4- to 6-ounce ramekins.

Combine the remaining ½ cup sugar, the egg, egg yolks, condensed milk, evaporated milk, vanilla, cream cheese, and salt in a blender, and blend until completely combined. Divide the mixture evenly among the ramekins.

Fill a large rectangular baking pan halfway with water. Carefully place the ramekins into the water in the pan, then place the pan on the center rack of the oven. Bake for about 40 to 50 minutes, until the centers of the custards are set.

Take the ramekins out of the water and let them cool to room temperature. Refrigerate for 4 hours or overnight.

Before serving, run a knife around the sides of the ramekins to loosen the flan. You can also dip the bottom halves of the ramekins in warm (not hot) water for about 30 seconds to ensure the bottom of the flan releases with ease. Invert the cups onto small plates.

Flan de Coco

Coconut Flan

Serves 6

What you'll need

¾ cup sugar

4 large eggs

2 large egg yolks

1 (14-ounce) can condensed milk

1 (14-ounce) can evaporated milk

1 teaspoon pure vanilla extract

¼ teaspoon salt

1 (17-ounce) can shredded coconut in heavy syrup, drained, with half of the syrup reserved

What you'll do

Preheat the oven to 325°F.

Heat ½ cup of the sugar in a small saucepan over medium-low heat for 5 to 6 minutes, stirring occasionally, until the sugar melts. Watch it closely so that it does not burn. Once the sugar has completely melted and turned a light caramel color, divide it evenly among six 4- to 6-ounce ramekins.

Combine the remaining ¼ cup sugar, the eggs, egg yolks, condensed milk, evaporated milk, vanilla, and salt in a blender, and blend until completely combined. Stir in half of the coconut, then pour the mixture into the ramekins. Because the coconut is heavier than the rest of the ingredients, it tends to sit at the bottom of the blender. Use a spoon to divide the coconut evenly among the ramekins, if necessary.

Fill a large rectangular baking pan halfway with water. Carefully set the ramekins in the water and place the pan on the center rack of the oven. Bake for about 40 to 50 minutes, until the centers of the custards are set.

Remove the ramekins from the water-filled pan and let them cool to room temperature. Refrigerate for at least 4 hours or up to overnight.

Before serving, run a knife around the sides of the ramekins to loosen the flan. You can also dip the bottom halves of the ramekins in some warm (not hot) water for about 30 seconds to ensure the bottom of the flan releases with ease. Invert the cups onto small plates.

Combine the remaining coconut with the reserved syrup.

To serve, place a dollop of the coconut mixture next to each flan.

Beverages

Cubans are not particularly fond of water as a beverage unless, of course, they are taking a pill prescribed by their cousin who was a doctor in Cuba. Generally, we do not favor water as an accompaniment to food. Wine is good, but unlike the Spaniards or French, it does not make an appearance on our dinner tables every day. Cubans do enjoy an occasional *fria* (literal translation: cold; Cuban slang: beer) now and again, but soft drinks and fruit shakes are generally our preference.

Soft drinks, like Coke and Pepsi, are popular, but many Cubans consume other less common soft drinks. Three in particular come to mind: *Jupiña, Materva,* and *Ironbeer.* These soft drinks are sweet and uniquely flavored. Sweet is important. After all, Cubans enjoy the pure sugarcane juice called *guarapo* regularly, which ironically is said to keep us regular. *Jupiña* is a pineapple-flavored soft drink. The name says it all "*Ju*" is short for *jugo* (juice), and "*piña*" means pineapple. Funny thing is that while it is delicious, this beverage probably has very little pineapple juice in it. *Materva* is flavored with *yerba mate,* a potent herb (popular in South America) that contains lots of caffeine. *Ironbeer* was always my little brother's favorite. You see, he was a ninety-pound weakling with a bodybuilder father and a sister who constantly taunted him. The can featured an impressive picture of a strong man flexing his rather large bicep. Naturally, my brother was certain that drinking this beverage in mass quantities would make him strong like, say, . . . iron? Instead, he was consuming so much caffeine, it had him bouncing off the walls (making him even more adorable).

I would hate to mislead anyone into believing that Cubans do not enjoy alcoholic beverages. We love beer, our mojitos, *Cuba Libres* (which literally translates as "free Cuba"). Give a Cuban a couple of mojitos, and he or she will be dancing to the beat of his or her own bongos.

Café con Leche

Cuban Coffee with Milk

Makes 1

Café con leche is one of those things that most Cubans cannot live without. It is as essential to us as anyone else's morning cup of joe and is definitely as addictive.

What you'll need

4 ounces whole milk

2 ounces evaporated milk

1 to 2 ounces prepared Cuban coffee or espresso

2 tablespoons sugar, or less according to taste (I like it sweet)

Small pinch of salt

What you'll do

Combine the whole milk and the evaporated milk in a small saucepan and bring to a boil. Pour the boiling milk into a large mug and add the coffee and sugar to taste. Add the tiniest pinch of salt.

Cuban Coffee with a Shot of Milk

The *cortadito* has always been a Cuban favorite and has become so popular in recent years that you can order it at almost any restaurant. A *cortadito* is a combination of Cuban espresso—*cafecito*—and a small amount of steamed milk. The milk is usually whole milk, evaporated milk, or a combination of the two, which I believe tastes best. Enjoy a steaming hot cup after a large meal as you sit back, pants let out (or completely unbuttoned), and doze off to the sound of your favorite *novela*.

What you'll need

3 ounces evaporated milk

3 ounces whole milk

6 ounces freshly prepared Cuban coffee or espresso

Sugar

What you'll do

Combine the evaporated milk and whole milk in a small saucepan and bring to a boil (you can do this in the microwave, but I promise you it will not taste the way it should). Watch it closely as it can easily boil over. Let stand a minute or two until a film forms on top of the milk. Skim off the film, pour the milk into 6 small cups, and top with coffee to achieve the desired darkness. Add sugar to taste.

Cafecito Cubano

Cuban Coffee

Makes 4 to 6

Cuban coffee is a sweet espresso drink made with strong, dark roast espresso sweetened with a thick sugar foam. Cafecito is a huge part of our Cuban culture. Cuban coffee is enjoyed for breakfast as part of your *café con leche*, after dessert, or anytime you need a little boost.

What you'll need

4 to 6 cup stovetop espresso maker

Classic silver bell creamer cup or any measuring cup

Ground espresso (I use Cuban ground coffee, of course, but any dark roast will do)

4 tablespoons sugar

What you'll do

Fill your espresso maker with water and ground espresso according to manufacturer's directions. Place on the stove at medium-high heat and brew the espresso.

Add the sugar to a Pyrex (liquid) measuring cup or creamer cup. Add the first few drops of espresso from the espresso maker into the cup of sugar. The first few drops of espresso that come out of the espresso maker are usually the most concentrated. That's what we want!

Allow the espresso maker to continue to brew. Meanwhile, stir the sugar and those few drops of espresso vigorously into a pale, thick sugar foam (*espumita*). If you've never done this before, there will be a bit of trial and error. I recommend you add a few drops of espresso at a time and stir until the sugar foam is thick but drippy.

Once the espresso maker is done brewing, pour the brewed espresso into the cup with the sugar foam. Stir together slowly to combine. Serve immediately in espresso cups.

Chocolate Caliente

Hot Chocolate

Serves 6

It is common knowledge that it does not get very cold in Miami. On the rare occasion when the temperature dips *way down* into the sixties, Cubans go out and get three things: a sweater, hot chocolate, and churros (page 145). No "cold" day in Miami is complete without a mug of wickedly rich and sweet Cuban-style hot chocolate.

In this recipe, I call for Menier sweet chocolate. Look for it in the baking section of your grocery store or where the powdered hot chocolate mixes are found. But if you can't find it, any sweetened baking chocolate will do.

What you'll need

½ cup evaporated milk

¼ cup sweetened condensed milk

1 (8-ounce) bar Menier sweet chocolate (see headnote), finely chopped

3 cups whole milk

Sugar

Pinch of salt

What you'll do

Combine the evaporated milk and condensed milk in a large saucepan and bring to a boil. Immediately reduce the heat to medium-low, then add the chocolate, stirring until it melts. Whisk in the whole milk 1 cup at a time. Add the salt. Cover the pan, reduce the heat to low, and simmer for 30 minutes. Add sugar to taste.

Café Bon Bon

Bon Bon Coffee

Makes 1

Popularized in Spain, café bon bon is a dessert in itself. It is sweet and decadent and a little too easy to make—which makes it even harder to resist.

What you'll need

2 shots espresso

2 to 3 tablespoons sweetened condensed milk (depending on how sweet you like it)

What you'll do

Brew the espresso according to manufacturer's directions, depending on which type of espresso maker you are using. This recipe works well with espresso pods, but you will need two for best results.

Pour the espresso into a glass cup.

Slowly drizzle in the condensed milk. It will sink to the bottom, making for a beautiful, layered presentation.

Serve immediately with a spoon.

Mamey Milkshake

Mamey is a tropical fruit native to Mexico and Central America, but it is also found in Cuba and Puerto Rico. It is football shaped with a rough skin and a red-orange, dense interior. The fruit is only available for a few months of the year, which is why its pulp is often sold frozen. You can find it online or in the Hispanic frozen food section of most large supermarkets.

There are two schools of thought when it comes to preparing mamey milkshakes: One advocates for using frozen mamey pulp as a base for the shake, the other votes for mamey ice cream. I provide you with directions for both options below. While both are delicious, I prefer to use frozen mamey pulp. You can also make the milkshake with fresh mamey by adding some ice and sugar to the recipe below.

What you'll need

Using frozen mamey pulp:

8 ounces whole milk (you know how I feel about skim milk)

4 ounces frozen mamey pulp

4 tablespoons sweetened condensed milk

Sugar, to taste

Using mamey ice cream

6 ounces whole milk

2 large scoops mamey ice cream

Sugar, to taste

What you'll do

Combine all the ingredients for either the mamey pulp or mamey ice cream version in a blender and blend until smooth and creamy. Serve immediately.

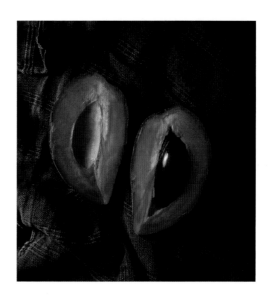

While sangria originated in Spain, it is quite popular among Cubans, almost certainly due to its sweetness. Be warned, the combination of ingredients is potent and will get you when you least expect it. You've been warned. Now drink up.

What you'll need

½ cup brandy (preferably Spanish)

1 cup lemonade

Juice of 1 orange (about ¼ cup)

2 tablespoons superfine sugar

1 (750 ml) bottle red table wine

½ cup soda water

1 orange, sliced

1 lemon, sliced

1 red apple, cored and cubed

Ice cubes

What you'll do

Combine the brandy, lemonade, orange juice, and sugar in a large pitcher and mix well. Add the wine, soda water, and fruit, and stir. Fill the pitcher halfway with ice cubes and serve immediately.

White Sangria

What you'll need

Ice cubes

½ cup triple sec

1 cup lemonade

Juice of 1 large lemon (about 3 tablespoons)

4 tablespoons superfine sugar

1 (750 ml) bottle white table wine

½ cup soda water

1 orange, sliced

1 lemon, sliced

1 green apple, cored and cubed

What you'll do

Combine the triple sec, lemonade, lemon juice, and sugar in a large pitcher and mix well. Add the wine, soda water, and fruit and stir. Fill the pitcher halfway with ice cubes and serve immediately.

Cuban-Style Mimosa

Makes 1

Mimosas and bellinis are great. But let's be real, they are a bit tired. This tropical version is a nice change of pace. Also works well served in a goblet with some ice, a lemon wedge, or a sprig of mint.

What you'll need

3 ounces chilled Champagne or prosecco

1 ounce guava juice

½ ounce passion fruit juice

What you'll do

In a champagne flute, combine the guava and passion fruit juice, stirring lightly. Top with chilled Champagne or prosecco.

Mula Estilo Cubano

Cuban-Style Mule

Makes 1

The Moscow mule continues to gain popularity at bars and restaurants. Which begs the question, if Moscow has a "mule," shouldn't Cuba have one too? This recipe is our answer to the traditional mule and it's delicious!

What you'll need

1½ ounces chilled vodka

3 ounces ginger beer

2 ounces guava juice

Lime wedge, for serving

What you'll do

Fill a glass or metal mug three-quarters of the way with ice. Add the guava juice and vodka and stir. Top with ginger beer and stir lightly. Serve with a squeeze of lime.

Daiquiri

The original daiquiri—made of rum, lime, and sugar—was created in Cuba in 1896 by an American mining engineer named Jennings Cox. He named the drink after the Cuban town of Daiquiri. Some say he ran out of gin and had to "make do" with rum. Hemingway was famous for drinking this classic concoction at El Floridita restaurant in Havana. It is said he often lingered at the bar for hours on end ordering doubles—later named *Papa Dobles*—which contained 4 full ounces of rum.

What you'll need

2 ounces light Bacardi rum

2 teaspoons superfine sugar

1 ounce fresh lime juice

1 tablespoon triple sec, optional

½ cup crushed ice

1 slice lime, for garnish

What you'll do

Combine the rum, sugar, lime juice, triple sec, and ice in a blender and blend for 20 to 30 seconds. Pour into a chilled glass and garnish with the lime slice. Serve immediately.

Mojito

Makes 1

This delicious and refreshing libation needs no introduction. It has become so popular that you can order it just about anywhere. Salud!

What you'll need

8 fresh mint leaves, plus more for garnish

2 teaspoons sugar

1 lime, juiced (about 3 tablespoons), plus lime slices for garnish

1½ ounces white rum

Splash of sparkling water or soda water

What you'll do

Combine the mint and sugar in a cocktail shaker. Use a muddler to crush the leaves together with the sugar. Add the lime juice and rum and shake well. Pour into a tall glass filled with ice. Top with the sparkling water and garnish with slices of lime and mint leaves.

ACKNOWLEDGMENTS

I dedicate this book to my first grandchild, Blair. Despite your physical absence, you are always with me and will forever occupy an enormous piece of my heart. Thank you for teaching me to be brave, and the lesson that in the midst of unthinkable sadness you can find true strength.

A huge thank-you to all the wonderful women who helped make this book possible. To the incredibly talented photographer Catalina Ayubi, you understood my vision from day one and ignored the misconception that Cuban food doesn't photograph well. You created magic through your impeccable lens. To Yuly Lopez, thank you for the beautiful food styling and for your amazing ability to make even a simple sandwich into a masterpiece.

Thank you to my mom, Ela Quincoces, for instilling in me a love of food and family, and for teaching me everything I know about Cuban food. To my daughters, Kati and Beba, nothing I have ever done would be remotely possible without you. Your constant encouragement and belief in my abilities is the fuel that feeds my soul. I am so grateful for the gift that you are.

Last but not least, to Sian and everyone at UPF, thank you for trusting in my work and making writing this book seem effortless.

GLOSSARY

Ajiaco: A hearty meat and vegetable stew.

Annatto: A red-orange food coloring and flavoring used in many Latin American cuisines. It's derived from the seeds of achiote trees and is a major ingredient in bijol and the Sazón spice blends by Goya Foods.

Bijol: See annatto.

Boniato: A type of sweet potato, commonly a called Cuban sweet potato.

Café con leche: Translated as "coffee with milk." A glass of Cuban coffee, or espresso, is served alongside a cup of steamed milk. The coffee is poured into the milk before drinking.

Calabaza: Commonly known as a Cuban squash, the calabaza is a hybrid between a pumpkin and a squash. It has green or yellow skin and yellow-orange flesh.

Chicharos: Split peas.

Chorizo: Spanish pork sausage, with a distinct red color that comes from paprika.

Congri: Red beans with rice.

Croqueta preparada: A Cuban sandwich with two ham croquettes added to the inside.

Cuban bread: Similar to French and Italian bread but made with lard instead of oil. It has a hard, thin, almost papery crust and a soft flaky middle. It is often baked with a long, moist palm frond on top of the loaves, which creates a shallow trench in the upper crust.

Cuban coffee: Espresso with sugar added during the brewing process.

Cortadito: Translated as "short one," this is a Cuban coffee topped with steamed milk.

Fabas: Butter beans or lima beans.

Fideos: Very thin noodles, similar to vermicelli or angel hair pasta.

Frijoles colorados: Red beans.

Guava: Guavas are a dense fruit with green skin and white to pink pulp. They can range from extremely sweet to tart, depending on their ripeness.

Harina: In Spanish, harina means flour. However, this term also refers to the cornmeal mixture known as masa harina that is used to make corn tortillas and tamales.

Jamón serrano: Spanish dry-cured ham, sliced thin, similar to Italian prosciutto.

Lacón: Dry-cured pork foreleg.

Lechón asado: Whole roasted pig.

Maduros: Fried sweet, or ripened, plantains.

Malanga: A root vegetable, similar to taro and cassava, with a woodsy taste.

Mamey: A tropical fruit with a light pink to deep salmon pulp and the flavor of sweet pumpkin with a hint of berry.

Mariquitas: Plantain chips.

Mojo: A signature marinade of Cuba made from garlic and sour orange juice.

Morcilla: Spanish blood pudding.

Moros: Black beans with rice, often called Moros y Cristianos (Moors and Christians).

Palomilla: Butterflied top sirloin steaks. A common cut of meat in Latin communities.

Picadillo: Cuban-style meat hash.

Pimentón: Smoked paprika, used to flavor Spanish chorizos and paella. Often comes in three varieties—sweet and mild (dulce), bittersweet and medium hot (agridulce), and hot (picante).

Sabor: Flavor, taste, spirit.

Sofrito: A fragrant sauce made of garlic, onion, tomato, and bell peppers that forms the base of many Cuban dishes.

Sour orange: Also known as bitter or Seville oranges, these oranges have a very tart juice and form the basis for many Cuban marinades and sauces.

Tamales: Cornmeal dough filled with a sweet or savory filling, then wrapped in corn husks or banana leaves and boiled or steamed.

Tasajo: Salt-cured and dried beef.

Tostones: Green (unripe) plantains that are cut into slices, fried, flattened, and fried again.

Valencia rice: Valencia rice takes its name from the Valencia province of Spain. Also known as Spanish, paella, or pearl rice, this is a short-grain rice.

Vino seco: A fortified dry cooking wine that is the one exception to the "not good enough to drink not good enough to cook with rule." It is a must for Cuban recipes but not the kind of wine you could even fathom drinking. It tastes like anti-freeze straight up but imparts a delicious and unique flavor to food.

Yuca: Also known as cassava, yuca is a starchy root vegetable similar in size and texture to the malanga. It has white flesh and a dark brown skin, and texture like a potato.

INDEX